AROUND THE WORLD CRAFTS
FOR CHURCH AND HOME

By
Susan Addington

Illustrated by
Gary Hoover

Cover by Kathryn R. Marlin

Copyright © 1994

Shining Star Publications

ISBN No. 1-56417-001-2

Standardized Subject Code TA ac

Printing No. 987654321

Shining Star Publications
1204 Buchanan St., Box 299
Carthage, IL 62321-0299

Unless otherwise indicated, the New International Version of the Bible was used in preparing the activities in this book.

DEDICATION

This book is dedicated to my family: my husband Tom, and my three children—Kimberly, Sally, and Joel.

Susan

TABLE OF CONTENTS

To the Teacher/Parent 4

Australia: Boomerang 5

Austria: Bookmark 7

Balkans: Bread Craft 8

Brazil: Climbing Snake 10

Canada: Stone Statues 11

China: Rice Is Nice 12

China: Vegetable and Fruit Prints 16

England: Rockers 18

Europe: Stained-Glass Windows 20

Europe: Quilling 22

Finland: Toothpick Frames 24

France: Neckerchief 25

Germany: Castles 26

Greece: Gingerbread 30

Hawaii: Whistles 32

Hong Kong: Homemade High Rises 33

Honduras: Turtle Racing 34

India: Stuffed Elephants 36

Iran: Papier-Mâché People 41

Italy: Pressed Flowers 43

Italy: Punch-and-Judy Puppets 44

Japan: Rice Bags 47

Java: Batik T-Shirts 49

Korea: Stone Games 51

Lapland: Arctic Scene 54

Lithuania and the Ukraine: Batik Eggs 57

Mexico: Rag Dolls 59

Nepal: Animated Books 61

Netherlands: Pinwheels 63

North America, South America, and Africa: Beads 64

Norway: Rosemaling 66

Pakistan: Mosaic 68

Panama: Covered Boxes 70

Peru: Jewelry 72

Philippines: Weavings 73

Poland: Paper Cutting 75

Poland: Carving 77

Portugal: Tiles 78

Saudi Arabia: Weavings 80

Scotland: Thistles 82

South America, North America, and Africa: Peace Paint 84

South and Central America: Baskets 85

Spain and Mexico: Piñata 87

Spain: Silhouettes 89

Sri Lanka: Sandals 90

Sweden: Heart Baskets 92

Switzerland: Candles 93

Syria: Sand Pouring 94

United States: Lanterns 96

TO THE TEACHER/PARENT

"For God so loved the world that he gave his one and only Son, that whoever believes in him shall not perish but have eternal life." (John 3:16) It is a privilege as teachers to allow students to see the unique world for which Jesus died. It is exciting to be a part of their seeing the creativity and knowledge outside their smaller world of home and community. It is an honor to help plant the seed of desire in their hearts to go and tell the world about the Savior who died for us all.

My desire is that these projects will be used to make lessons sparkle as children are taught about missions in the rest of the world, and about concepts such as God our fortress (castles), Jesus the Light of the World (candle), resting in the shadow of the Almighty (silhouettes), and the peace of God (peace paint).

The projects in *Around the World Crafts for Church and Home* may be done by one or more youngsters at home or in group settings such as Christian day school, Sunday schools, children's clubs. A biblical teaching suggestion is included with each craft to help children learn an important concept or value related to their activity.

Before starting any project, read carefully through the instructions with the children to be sure they understand them. Take time to study together the illustrations and the list of materials.

Many of these projects require materials commonly found in most households or classrooms. Other projects may require trips to craft shops or other specialty stores to purchase some inexpensive supplies.

Encourage children to do as much as possible themselves, according to their particular ages and abilities. Many projects can be done quite simply with only a few basic materials, but optional materials and ideas are provided for those youngsters who wish to spend more time and energy decorating their projects. Variations are sometimes suggested as alternatives based on the original ideas. Helpful hints are included with many of the projects to make them easier to do.

Try to intervene only as necessary, such as to make copies of patterns or to help children trace patterns. Instructions will also indicate when an adult's help is definitely recommended for safety reasons, such as when using a sharp hobby knife or hot iron.

SS3823

Australia

BOOMERANG
Fly with a round-trip ticket every time!

The Australians were the first to develop a device shaped to follow a controlled path through the air. The early bushmen used it in hunting, and it is still used today. Our boomerang will be a different kind—good for a small room on a rainy day!

MATERIALS:
Pattern (page 6)
One side of a medium-sized cereal box
Pencil
Scissors

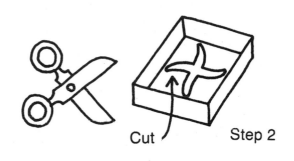

Cut   Step 2

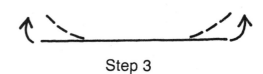

Step 3

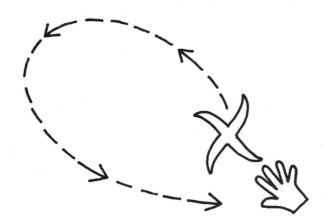

INSTRUCTIONS:
1. Cut out the pattern on page 6.
2. Trace pattern on the plain side of cutout cereal box and cut it out.
3. Bend a smooth upward curve in the tip of each arm. (This will hold it upright and keep it moving steadily.)
4. Throw the boomerang like a Frisbee™. Remember, practice makes perfect.

BIBLICAL TEACHING:
We cannot get rid of our sins by ourselves; they come right back to us. We do them over and over again. Only God can permanently remove our sins. Read Psalm 103:11-12.

SS3823

Austria

BOOKMARK
A bookmark for a friend

Edelweiss, a lovely white flower found in the Alps, has always been a very special gift to give. Because edelweiss is usually found in high, rocky crevices, only a very dedicated friend would climb for it to give it away.

MATERIALS:
Wildflowers (picked only in unrestricted spots like ditches or your own private property, please)
Phone book
Envelope with clear window
Construction paper
Scissors
Glue
Markers

INSTRUCTIONS:
1. Pick a flower you would like to use or one that reminds you of edelweiss.
2. Press it flat in a phone book and leave it to dry for five to eight days.
3. Cut around the window part of an envelope leaving the corner intact.
4. Cut a colored piece of paper a little smaller and slide it in between the layers.
5. Glue your flower carefully in place with a small amount of glue so that it shows through the window.
6. Seal the edges of the open sides of the envelope.
7. Decorate with markers.
8. Give to a friend and explain the specialness of edelweiss.

BIBLICAL TEACHING:
If God cares for the tiniest flowers, like edelweiss, how much more He cares for you and me! Read Matthew 6:28-30, 33.

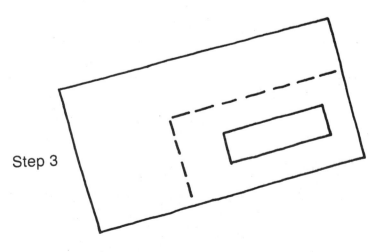

Step 3

The Balkans

BREAD CRAFT
Bread is for the wall not just to eat!

The Balkan peninsula is populated with Greeks, Slavs, Bulgarians, and Albanians, to name a few. Sculptured bread has played an important role in holiday celebrations throughout history on this peninsula which juts out into the Mediterranean Sea. There are many fun ways to do bread sculpture. Give it a try.

BASIC ART BREAD DOUGH

MATERIALS:
4 cups flour
1 cup salt
$1\frac{1}{2}$ cups warm water
Mixing bowl
Mixing spoon
Water in a spray bottle
Cookie sheet
Varnish or acrylic paint, paintbrush (optional)
Plastic bag or container with lid

INSTRUCTIONS:
1. Mix salt and flour together.
2. Add water and knead the dough until smooth.
3. Keep dough in plastic bag or lidded container when not using.
4. Shape as desired and put on cookie sheet. If connecting parts, use water on your fingers like glue to help in smoothing out surface.
5. Spray with water for a toastier appearance.
6. Bake in a 300°F oven for $2\frac{1}{2}$ hours.
7. When cool, varnish or paint with acrylic (optional).

IDEAS FOR SHAPES:
Your name, a short saying, a face, or an animal.

HOW TO USE SHAPES:
Glue on a piece of wood for a plaque, poke a paper clip into shape before baking to hang on a string, or put a magnet on back for hanging on the refrigerator.

BIBLICAL TEACHING:
Bread is important for food, but it is not the most important thing in our lives. Our faith in God and our relationship with Him matters more. Read Deuteronomy 8:1-3.

BAKER'S CLAY

MATERIALS:
1-pound package of baking soda
1 cup of cornstarch
1$\frac{1}{4}$ cups of cold water
Saucepan
Fork
Rolling pin
Cookie cutters
Waxed paper
Food coloring, small paintbrushes (optional)
Spoon
Cloth
Plate

INSTRUCTIONS:
1. Combine baking soda and cornstarch in saucepan.
2. Add water and mix with fork until smooth.
3. ADULT SUPERVISION NEEDED: Cook one minute over medium heat.
4. Spoon onto plate and cover with a damp cloth. Cool.
5. Roll out on waxed paper and cut into desired shapes with cookie cutters.
6. Dry for at least 24 hours.
7. Paint with food coloring (optional).
Note: This dough is white when dried without painting.

SPICY DOUGH ART

MATERIALS:
Equal amounts of cinnamon and applesauce
Rolling pin
Cookie cutters
Cookie sheet
Mixing bowl
Spoon

INSTRUCTIONS:
1. Mix cinnamon and applesauce well in mixing bowl.
2. Roll out on surface that has been sprinkled with cinnamon.
3. Cut into desired shapes with cookie cutters.
4. Bake at 300°F for 2 hours or until crisp.
Note: This dough art is great for Christmas tree ornaments but after baking needs to be stored in tight container for long-term storage.

Shining Star Publications, Copyright © 1994

SS3823

Brazil

CLIMBING SNAKE
A climbing snake in a palm tree!

Brazil is a South American jungle-filled country known for its variety of wild animals. Snakes are a common sight. You can make a snake that will climb a tree whenever you like!

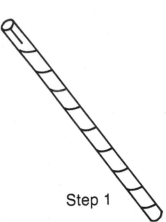

Step 1

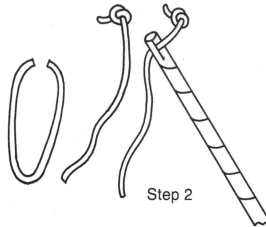

Step 2

MATERIALS:
Straw
Scissors
Green chenille stems
4" black chenille stem
Rubber band
Hot glue gun and glue sticks
Pencil

INSTRUCTIONS:
1. Cut four small slits ¹/₂" deep in the top of the straw.
2. Tie a knot in the end of a split rubber band and put through slit in the straw.
3. ADULT SUPERVISION NEEDED: Add a little glue where rubber band is in slit.
4. Fold two green chenille stems in half and make shapes of leaves at each end.
5. Twist the two chenille stems together and place in slits in crosswise fashion.
6. Add a few drops of glue at top of slits.
7. Twist the black chenille stem around your finger or a pencil, and tie one end of the rubber band to the snake. (You may have to adjust the rubber band to make it small enough so that the snake will spring up the tree.) Add glue to secure tie in rubber band. Let dry and put snake on the palm tree.

Step 4

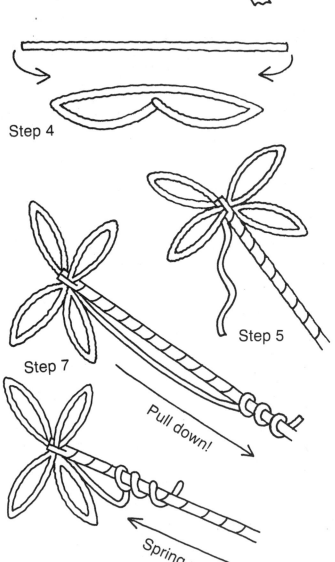

Step 5

Step 7

Pull down!

Spring up!

BIBLICAL TEACHING:
Think of all the interesting animals God created! He made each one different from the others with special abilities and instincts. Read Genesis 1:24-25.

SS3823

Canada

STONE STATUES
Create stone statues!

Canada has a seacoast that includes over 36,000 miles of mainland and over 115,000 miles of islands. Children throw stones into the water to hear the splash. They also pile stones and use their imaginations creatively. Collect some stones yourself and be creative!

PEBBLE PEOPLE

MATERIALS:
Smooth stones—big and small
Glue
Acrylic paint
Paintbrush
Clear nail polish

INSTRUCTIONS:
1. Stack and glue stones and pebbles in shapes like people and animals.
2. Paint on features with acrylic paint.
3. For a shiny finish use clear nail polish when other paint is dry.

OTHER IDEAS:
1. Build stone walls and fences for your pebble people.
2. Cover cans with glue and small pebbles.
3. Write a saying on a smooth, flat stone. Polish it and glue a magnet on the back for hanging on the refrigerator.

BIBLICAL TEACHING:
Long ago, a young boy who had faith in God defeated a giant with a smooth stone and a slingshot! Do you know who he was? Read 1 Samuel 17.

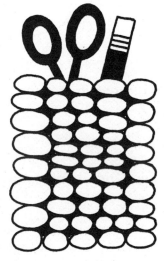

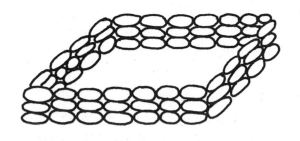

RICE IS NICE!
Thanks to the farmers in the paddies!

China is a very large country with a very large population. Two-thirds of its population is involved in agriculture. One of the chief crops is rice, and that's nice because it is a staple in the Chinese diet. With a few pieces of paper and some yarn, you can make a costume much like the clothes a Chinese farmer might wear in the rice paddies.

MATERIALS:
Patterns (pages 13-15)
Black yarn
Construction paper
Glue
Scissors
Yarn
Hole punch
Pencil
Markers
Ruler

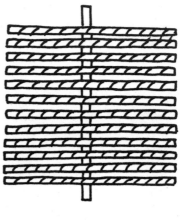

Step 3

INSTRUCTIONS:
1. Cut out pattern A on page 13.
2. Cut 40 pieces of yarn into strips of 20" each.
3. Glue the center of each piece of yarn to the pattern spreading out to cover the pattern to make a black wig.
4. Cut out pattern B on page 14, and trace onto two pieces of same color of paper.
5. Overlap the long tabs to make a complete circle.
6. Glue at the tabs, leaving a slit from center to edge.
7. When glue is dry, overlap sides of the slit to make a hat with a slight conical shape.
8. Glue the wig to inside of hat.
9. Make a copy of pattern C, page 15, and color brightly.
10. Fold to make a crease and cut on lines.
11. Open again and roll into a tube shape overlapping the edges and gluing in place.
12. Make holes and tie yarn to top of lantern.

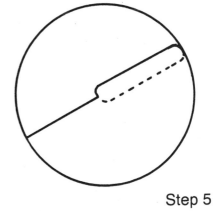

Step 5

To complete your costume of hat, hair, and lantern, you could dress in solid-colored, two-piece pajamas and wear white socks with thong-type slippers.

BIBLICAL TEACHING:
People all over the world, including the Chinese, need Jesus. God wants us to take His message to them. Read Matthew 28:19-20.

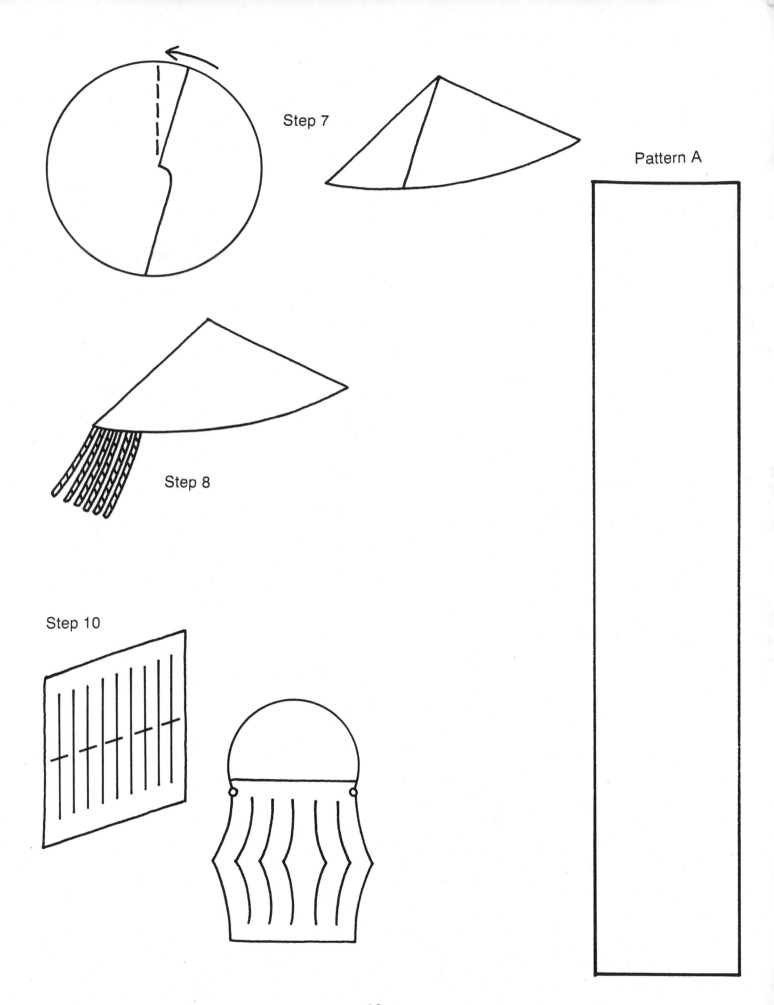

Step 7

Pattern A

Step 8

Step 10

SS3823

Pattern B

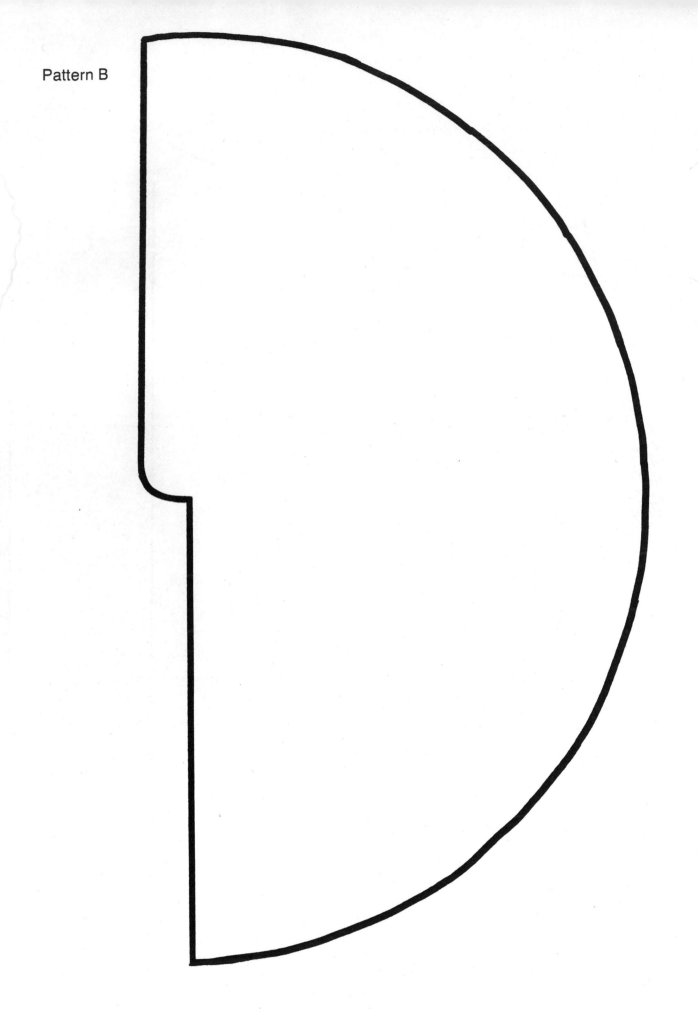

SS3823

Pattern C

Apply glue here.

_____

_____

_____

_____

_____

_____

_____

_____

China

VEGETABLE AND FRUIT PRINTS
Vegetables and fruits are good for a healthy heart and wonderful art!

The clever Chinese not only invented kites and firecrackers; in the tenth century, they started doing block printing. Although they used wood for their stamps, we'll try making ours from softer material–vegetables or fruits!

MATERIALS:
White paper
Fabric paints
Whipped cream containers
Vegetables and fruits of different shapes and sizes (green peppers, mushrooms, apples, cauliflower, carrots)
Kitchen knives

Carrot

INSTRUCTIONS:
1. ADULT SUPERVISION NEEDED: Cut vegetables or fruits in half.
2. Put different colors of fabric paint in containers. Lids may be used as blotters.
3. Dip "stamp" into paint and touch on "blotter" to make sure it is even.
4. Use your "stamps" to make people, flowers, animals, or designs.

VARIATIONS:
1. Use stamps on corners of recipe cards for a Mother's Day gift.
2. Use stamps on folded paper for making stationery or cards. Decorate corners of plain white envelopes to match.
3. Make wrapping paper by stamping freezer paper or package wrap.
4. Use stamps to decorate a T-shirt or apron.
Remember to have newspapers or a paper bag under the cloth when you paint.

Mushroom

RECIPE

BIBLICAL TEACHING:
Did you know that God has put His special seal or "stamp" on every Christian? His "stamp" is the Holy Spirit, who helps us show the world that we belong to Jesus. Read Ephesians 1:13-14.

SS3823

Apple Without Seeds

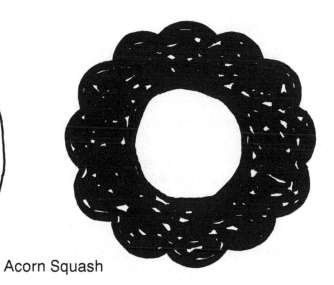

Acorn Squash

SS3823

England

ROCKERS
Soothing rockers and cradles, or are they beds for bawling babies and bucking horses?

Rocking toys were amusing English children before the first English colonists sailed to the New World. An inventive American took the rocking idea and relaxing adult rocking chairs were soon being enjoyed. You can make these rockers and cradles to hold small treasures.

MATERIALS:
Patterns (page 19)
Light tagboard or cereal box sides
Small box without top, such as empty check box (top or bottom) or individual size milk carton with top
  cut off
Markers or crayons
Scissors
Glue
Fabric or paint (optional)

INSTRUCTIONS:
1. Cut out two of either pattern on page 19. Color both brightly.
2. Glue onto light tagboard and trim around the edge.
3. Glue side of box to back of pattern. Glue other pattern to other side of box, making it as even as possible with the opposite side.
4. Cover or paint box ahead of time for a more finished look (optional).

BIBLICAL TEACHING:
A cradle or rocking chair may help us rest, but true rest is found only in the Lord. Read Matthew 11:28-29.

Step 3

SS3823

STAINED-GLASS WINDOWS
"Stains" that you want to keep?

Stained-glass windows have been around for over 700 years. Some of those early works of art can be viewed in European cathedrals built in the Middle Ages. Here are two ways to duplicate that same combination of light and color filling a window.

ROUND WINDOW HANGER

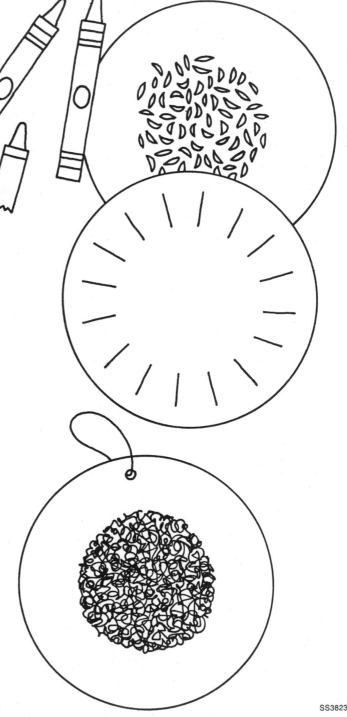

MATERIALS:
White coffee filters
Crayons (broken ones are fine)
Dull knife
Iron
Hole punch
Yarn or string
Paper towels or grocery bag

INSTRUCTIONS:
1. Peel paper from crayons.
2. Choose three or four colors that compliment each other.
3. Chop or shave little pieces of each crayon into a coffee filter.
4. Place another filter directly on top.
5. Place these two filters carefully between two pieces of thick paper towels or inside a flattened grocery bag.
6. ADULT SUPERVISION NEEDED: Iron until the crayons are melted.
7. Make a hole at the top and add a loop of yarn or string.

BIBLICAL TEACHING:
A stained-glass window or ornament becomes beautiful when light shines through it. When we let God's light shine through our lives, people see and want to know Him too. Read Matthew 5:14-16.

SS3823

OIL AND MARKER SPARKLER

MATERIALS:
Typing paper
Markers
Vegetable oil or baby oil
Margarine tub
Cotton ball
Clear plastic bag
Scissors
Hole punch
Yarn or string
Tape

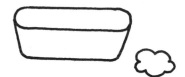

Step 3

INSTRUCTIONS:
1. Cut paper to fit inside the plastic bag.
2. Draw a picture on the paper, trying to fill it with color.
3. When you are done, dip a cotton ball in oil that has been poured in a margarine tub. Rub it over the entire picture.
4. Slide the picture inside the bag and seal with tape.
5. Punch a hole at the top center, and add a loop of string for easy hanging.

Step 4

QUILLING
Sit still? Learn a skill? Try to quill!

Quilling, also called paper filigree, is the art of rolling, bending, and creasing narrow strips of paper into coils and scrolls, and then assembling them into colorful pictures. These pieces of paper were at one time rolled on bird quills. This European art dates back to the fifteenth century when nuns used quilling to skillfully decorate religious articles. Let's try the skill of quilling!

MATERIALS:
Patterns (page 23)
Construction paper
Scissors
Ruler
Toothpicks
Waxed paper
Glue that dries clear
Margarine tub
Sponge (dampened)
Straight pins
Cardboard (2" x 2")
Stapler

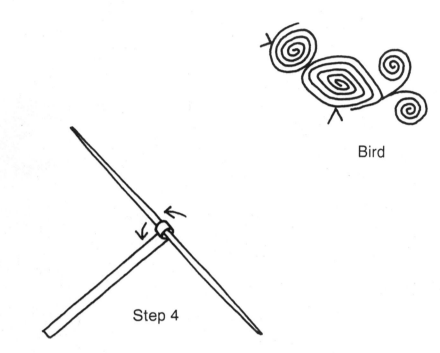

Bird

Step 4

INSTRUCTIONS:
1. Cut paper into strips $1/8$" wide and 8" long.
2. Put patterns on top of cardboard with waxed paper over the top and staple or pin in place. This is your guide for the quilling shapes.
3. Put some glue in a margarine tub.
4. Roll paper strips on a toothpick, and then fold or pinch as instructed on pattern. Put on glue with tip of a toothpick.
5. When glue is dry on shapes, put together for a larger picture.
   Note: The dampened sponge is for keeping your fingers free of dirt and stickiness from the glue. The pins hold the shapes in place while they dry.

BIBLICAL TEACHING:
As we shape and mold paper into objects of beauty, God wants to shape and mold us into new creations who will bring praise to Him. Read 2 Corinthians 5:17.

Mouse

Pattern Guide

Coils:

Tight Coil–Roll and then glue outside end without letting it unwind.

Loose Coil–Roll and then let it unwind to the size you want and glue the outside end.

Diamond–Roll a loose coil and pinch opposite sides between thumb and forefinger. Pinch only one side for leaf shape.

Scrolls:

Double Scroll–Roll both ends loosely toward the center on the same side of the paper strip.

S-Shaped Scroll–Roll both ends to the center on opposite sides of the strip.

V-Shaped Scroll–Fold the strip in half and roll both ends to the outside.

Heart–Fold the strip in half and roll both ends to the inside until they meet.

Relaxed Scroll–Roll a loose coil and stretch the outside end to the desired length.

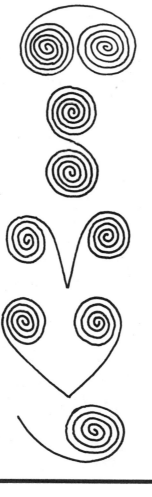

Christmas Tree

Flower

SS3823

Finland

TOOTHPICK FRAMES
Fun Finnish Frames

In Finland, one of the cold Scandinavian countries in northern Europe, wood is called "Green Gold." Finnish wood is used for everything from toothpicks to toys. With toothpicks you can make a real work of art!

MATERIALS:
Toothpicks (flat-sided work best)
Magazines, old greeting cards, or photographs
Glue
String, ribbon, or yarn
Scissors

INSTRUCTIONS:
1. Start with two toothpicks lying parallel with each other, a little closer than the length of a toothpick.
2. Place two more toothpicks on top, as if building a miniature log cabin, gluing where they overlap.
3. Repeat with two or three more layers, changing the direction of toothpicks each time. Let glue dry completely.
4. Find a picture that is small enough to fit into the toothpick frame.
5. Cut out the picture and glue to back of toothpick frame.
6. To create a hanger, glue a loop of string, ribbon, or yarn to the back.

BIBLICAL TEACHING:
Toothpicks are just little pieces of wood. They don't seem to be worth much, but they have many uses. The little things we do are important too. Little is much when God is in it. Read Colossians 3:17.

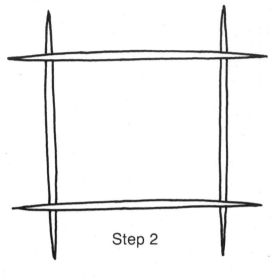

Step 2

Steps 5 and 6

SS3823

France

NECKERCHIEF
Art that is fit to be tied!

Men have used neck decorations for many centuries, but the cravat, the forerunner of today's tie, dates back to the seventeenth century. By decorating a simple handkerchief, you can make something similar.

MATERIALS:
White handkerchief
Crayons, fabric markers, or fabric paint bottles
Iron
Pencil
Paper
Paper bag or newsprint

INSTRUCTIONS:
1. ADULT SUPERVISION NEEDED: Press handkerchief out flat.
2. Sketch your ideas on a piece of paper first. Use big shapes.
3. Choose one of these three techniques.
   A. Markers: Use fabric markers so your design will be permanent. Make sure your cloth is on newsprint so it won't leak on the table.
   B. Crayons: Press hard and color brightly. Make the design permanent by placing it flat between pieces of paper bag and pressing it with a warm iron to melt the crayon design on the handkerchief.
   C. Fabric paint: Use paint bottles like squeezable paint pens to make designs. Put cloth on newsprint so it won't leak on table. Let it dry thoroughly before touching.

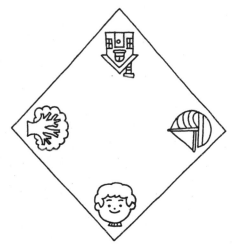

IDEAS FOR WEARING:
1. Fold in half, tie in back with corner hanging down, cowboy style.
2. Fold in half, tie in front, Boy Scout and Girl Scout style.
3. Fold in half two times. Tuck into pocket. Let a portion hang out.
4. Use your scarf for a hair bow or headband, Indian style.

BIBLICAL TEACHING:
It's fun to wear attractive clothes and colorful accessories, but God says what we're like on the inside is more important than what we look like on the outside. Read 1 Peter 3:3-4.

Germany

CASTLES
Strong fortresses of long ago!

Germany is a land of beauty with ancient castles sitting atop hills and mountains. These castles vary in shape and size but most are strong fortresses of stone. You can make miniature castles that have walls of "strong" Styrofoam™ or cardboard!

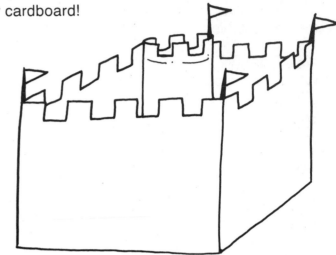

MATERIALS:
Patterns (pages 27-29)
Scissors
Pen or pencil
Styrofoam™, cardboard, or tagboard
Straws and/or toothpicks
Paper
Glue or tape

INSTRUCTIONS:
1. Cut out patterns A and B on pages 27 and 28. Trace two of each pattern on Styrofoam™ or cardboard.
2. Cut out these pieces and interlock the narrow slits to put pieces together.
3. If using tagboard, cut out pattern C on page 29. Trace for making a tower.
4. Bend into a tube shape and glue on edge.
5. Glue the tower into one corner, or create additional towers for two, three, or four corners.
6. Make small triangles to glue to straws or toothpicks. Tape or glue to walls and towers as flags.

BIBLICAL TEACHING:
God wants to be our fortress. We can run to Him when we are in trouble, and He will protect us and help us. Read Psalm 59:9, 16-17.

Step 2

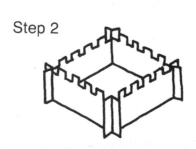

Step 6

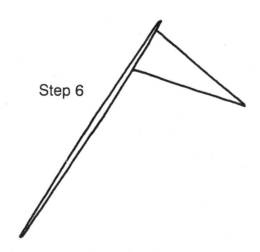

SS3823

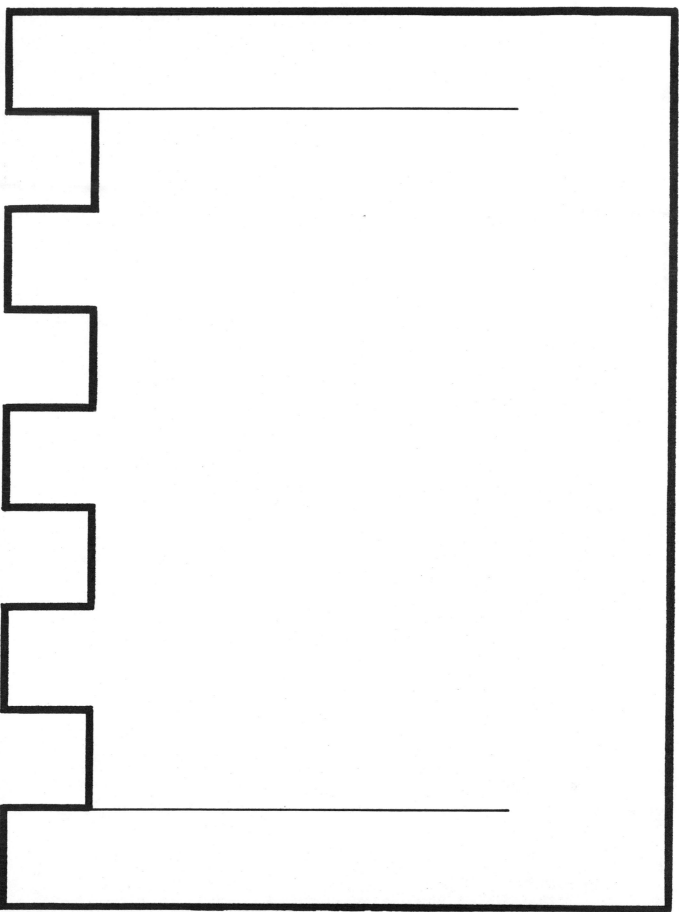

Cut 2

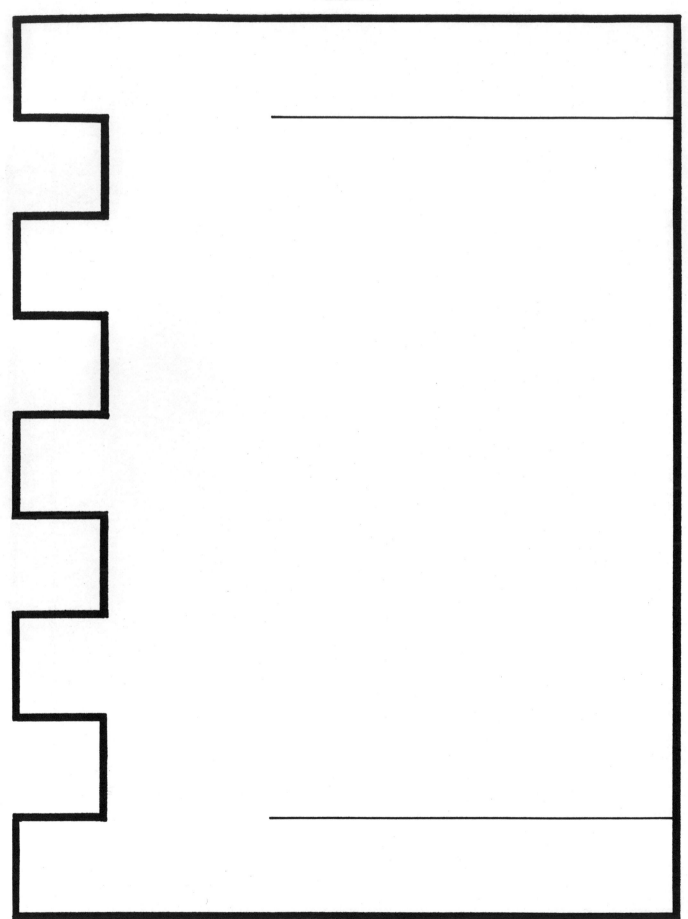

Cut 2

SS3823

Pattern C

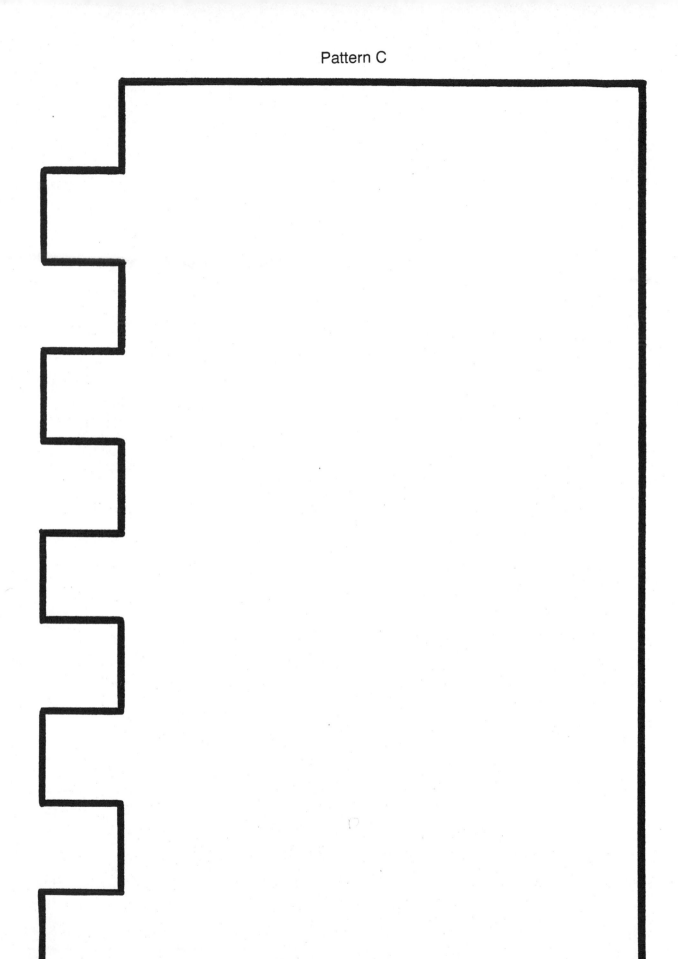

Glue on this edge.

SS3823

GINGERBREAD
Some spice that is nice!

The first recipe for this spicy cake came from Greece, where it was reportedly devised by a baker on the island of Rhodes about 2400 B.C. Here are two ways to try a gingerbread activity.

EASY MICROWAVE GINGERBREAD CAKE

INGREDIENTS:
1½ cups unsifted all-purpose flour
½ cup sugar
¾ teaspoon baking soda
½ teaspoon ginger
½ teaspoon cinnamon
½ teaspoon salt
½ cup cooking oil
1 egg
½ cup molasses
½ cup hot tap water

INSTRUCTIONS:
1. Mix dry ingredients.
2. Mix oil, egg, and molasses; add to dry ingredients, stirring well.
3. Add water and stir well.
4. Pour batter into 8" square microwave-safe pan.
5. Microwave on high for 7 to 9 minutes. This may vary according to microwave strength.
6. When cake is done, let cool.
7. Serve with whipped cream or sprinkled with powdered sugar.

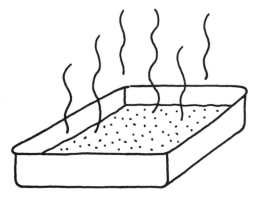

BIBLICAL TEACHING:
We all like a sweet treat now and then. Did you know that God's Word is also sweet? Read Psalm 119:103-104. Why do you think the Psalm writer said God's Word tasted sweet?

SS3823

EASY "GINGERBREAD" HOUSES

MATERIALS:
Small boxes of varying shapes and sizes such as cracker boxes, shoe boxes, and cheese boxes
Glue (hot glue can be used for speedy work with close adult supervision)
Graham crackers
Light poster board or shirt box cardboard
White commercial icing in squeeze tubes
Aluminum foil
Assortment of small candies (peppermints, M & M's™, gumdrops, etc.)
Cardboard base cut from side of cardboard box
Polyester fiberfill
Scissors

INSTRUCTIONS:
1. Glue crackers to sides of box, covering completely.
2. Cut a piece of light cardboard the length of the roof. Make it wide enough to fold like a peaked roof. Fold this in half, also folding the edges under to help make a convenient gluing ridge.
3. Glue roof on and cover with crackers.
4. Trim all edges with white icing lines.
5. Cut windows from aluminum foil and glue on.
6. Use candies to decorate around windows and make door shapes, etc.
7. For winter project, glue house to heavier base and surround with fiberfill snowdrifts. Make an aluminum foil pond.

Step 1

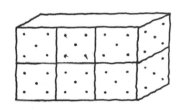

Step 2

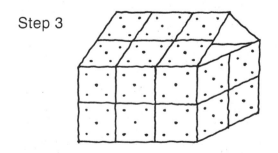

Fold

Edge glued to top of box.

Step 3

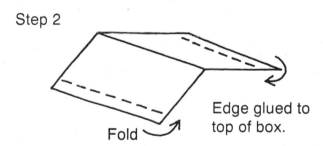

Step 7

Hawaii

WHISTLES
Whistle Away!

A natural toy used as a whistle by some in Hawaii is a ti leaf whistle. Since we have no ti leaves on the mainland, let's try making a whistle with paper and tape.

MATERIALS:
Pattern on this page
Tape
Scissors

INSTRUCTIONS:
1. Cut out the long strip.
2. Roll the strip keeping it very tight.
3. Fasten with tape.
4. Press the roll so that it changes from a round shape to an oval shape.
5. Blow hard. Don't squeeze so hard that the air cannot get through.

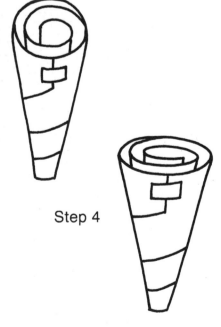

Steps 2 and 3

Step 4

SS3823

Hong Kong
HOMEMADE HIGH RISES

Because Hong Kong is the most densely populated city in the whole world, at approximately 250,000 people per square mile, it is filled with construction sites for high-rise apartment buildings. Try your own hand at building a miniature scaffolding or building frame.

MATERIALS:
Whole dry peas or beans
Toothpicks
Cardboard

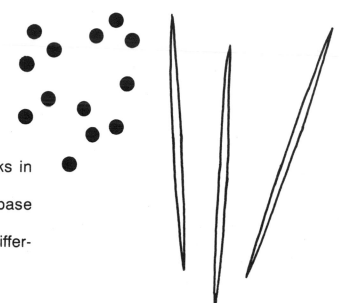

INSTRUCTIONS:
1. Soak peas overnight.
2. Use peas as joints between toothpicks in making a building structure.
3. Place finished project on cardboard base for thorough drying and transporting.
4. After it dries, add cardboard floors at different levels.

BIBLICAL TEACHING:
The Bible tells a story about the importance of the right foundation when building a house or a life. Read it in Matthew 7:24-27.

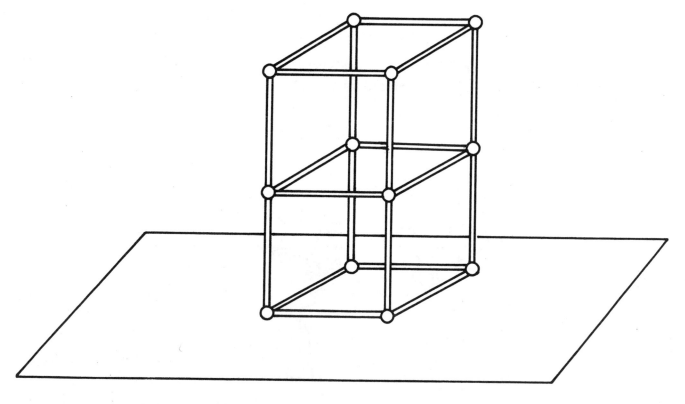

Honduras

TURTLE RACING

Honduras, a country in Central America, has an abundance of turtles. Do you think children there ever capture, name, and race them? Make a paper turtle and race it against your friends' turtles.

MATERIALS:
Light cardboard
Markers
String or yarn (in 10' lengths)
Scissors
Glue

INSTRUCTIONS:
1. Color and cut out turtle pattern on page 35, and write its name on its back.
2. Glue to light cardboard and trim around edges.
3. Poke string hole below the head.
4. Tie one end of the string to a chair rung or table leg.
5. Thread the string through the hole in the turtle as shown.
6. Pull tightly and the turtle will stand.
7. Release and he'll flop forward.
8. Repeat over and over for a great race.

BIBLICAL TEACHING:
How do you think the Christian life is like a race? What is the prize at the end of our race? Read Hebrews 12:1-3.

SS3823

India

STUFFED ELEPHANTS

India is very heavily populated by people, but not so crowded that there isn't enough room for plenty of elephants. It's easy to make a pillow shaped like an elephant.

MATERIALS:
Patterns (pages 39-40)
Scissors
Fabric
Straight pins
Yarn
Buttons
Crayon, marker, or tailor's chalk
Polyester fiberfill
Needle
Thread
Pencil

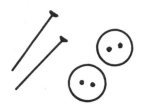

Step 2

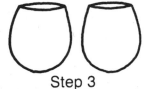

Step 3

INSTRUCTIONS:
1. Cut out patterns on pages 39-40, trace on back of fabric with crayon, tailor's chalk, or marker, and cut out.
2. To make ears, wrong sides together, sew $1/4$" from the edge leaving the flat side open.
3. Turn the ears right side out.
4. Make a tail by braiding three 6" pieces of yarn and tying a knot at both ends.
5. Lay one side of the body right side up. Place both ears on top of each other at top of elephant (step 5). Lay the tail at back of elephant with a little hanging over outer edge. Pin other side of elephant body with wrong side up.
6. Sew $1/4$" from edge around elephant, leaving the top edge open.
7. Turn right side out, using eraser end of pencil to gently spread out trunk and legs.
8. Stuff with fiberfill and slipstitch opening.
9. Sew on buttons for eyes.

Step 4

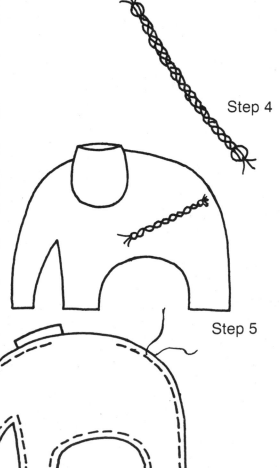

Step 5

Step 6

SS3823

STUFFED PAPER ELEPHANT

MATERIALS:
Patterns (pages 38 and 40)
Wallpaper
Yarn
Glue
Markers or crayons
Scissors
Tissues
Pencil

INSTRUCTIONS:
1. Cut out patterns, trace on wrong side of wallpaper, and cut out.
2. Lay out flat one side of elephant with wrong side up.
3. Put ears right sides together and glue on the flat edge.
4. Glue them on the elephant's head, standing straight up with the flat edge coming down under the edge slightly.
5. Braid three 6" pieces of yarn together, tying a knot at both ends.
6. Glue it at the back of the elephant with a little coming in over the edge.
7. Wad up six tissues. Place them evenly around the elephant's body, gluing lightly in place.
8. Take the other body part (right side up) and place on tissue part, gluing the edges securely.
9. Fold an ear down on both sides and draw two eyes.

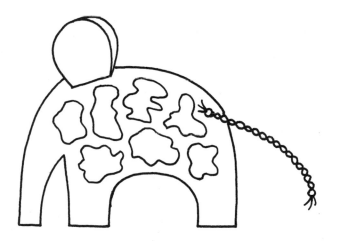

Steps 4, 6, and 7

Step 9

(Note: Tail and ears are connected
a little differently on this elephant.)

SS3823

Paper Elephant Pattern

Cut 2

SS3823

Elephant Pillow Pattern

Cut 2

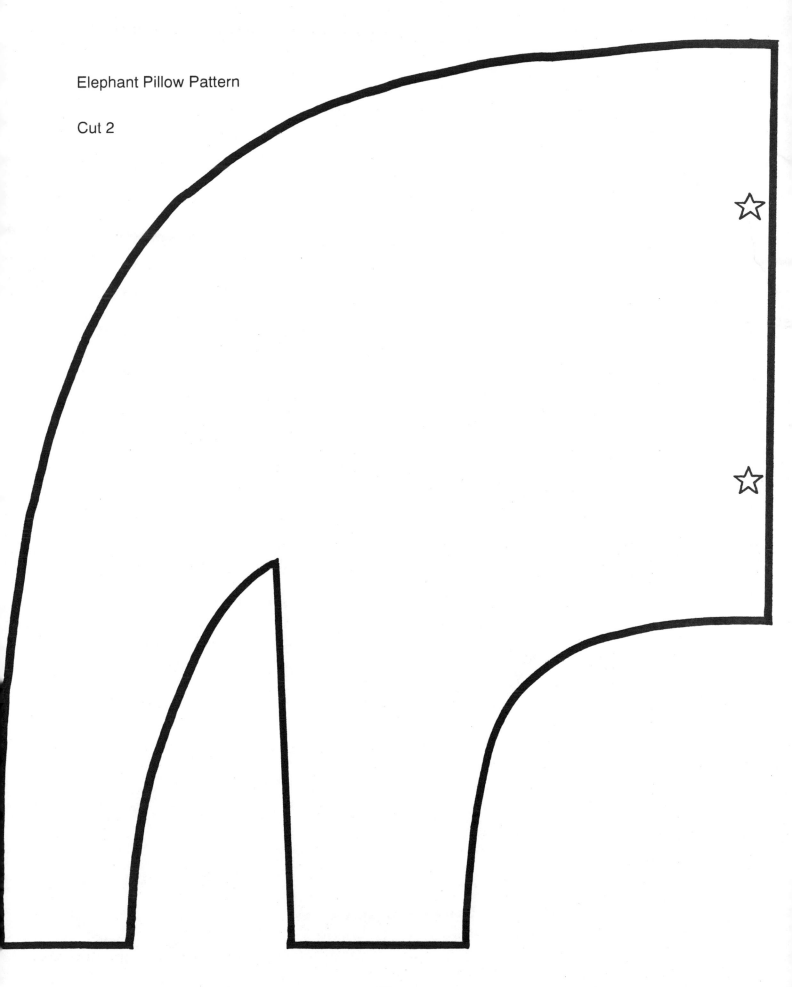

SS3823

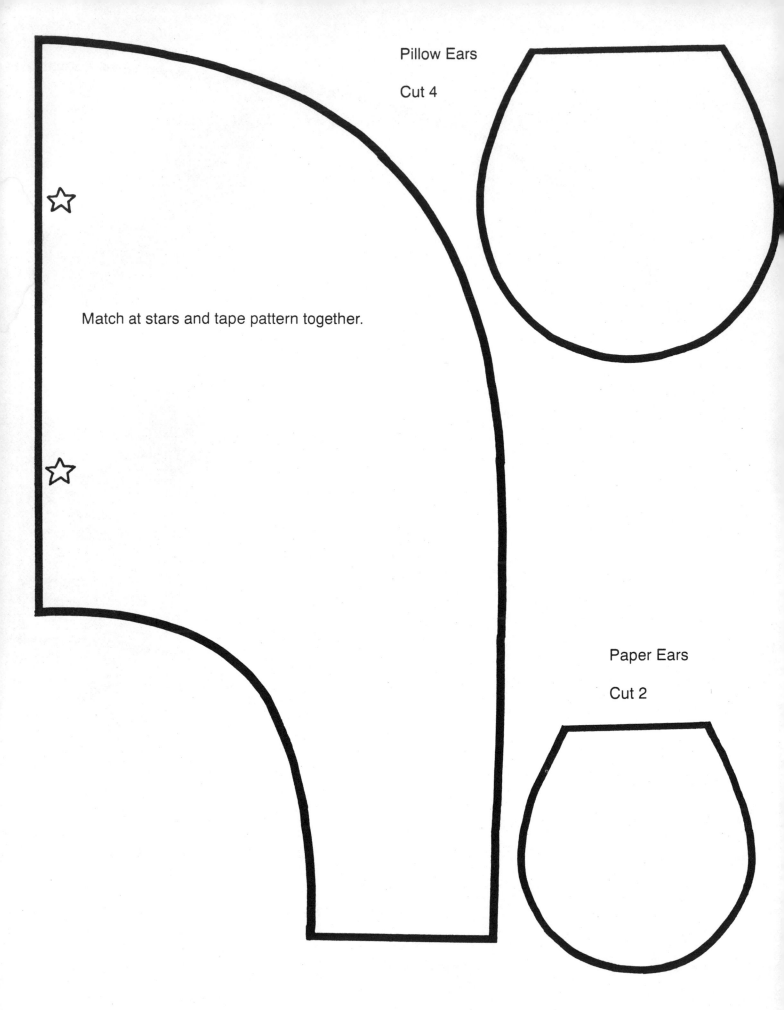

Pillow Ears

Cut 4

Match at stars and tape pattern together.

Paper Ears

Cut 2

SS3823

Iran

PAPIER-MÂCHÉ PEOPLE
Make people from household odds and ends!

Iran, once called Persia, is about the size of Alaska. Papier-mâché has been used there for centuries by craftsmen. Use bottles to make papier-mâché people.

MATERIALS:
Bottle
Newspapers
Papier-mâché mix
Water
A large container for mixing
Stirrer
Yarn
Glue
Construction paper
Poster or acrylic paint
Paintbrush
Scissors
Decorative items
Blender (optional)

INSTRUCTIONS:
1. Wash bottle inside and out. If necessary, soak in hot water to remove label.
2. Cover all working areas with newspapers. A layer of waxed paper or a vinyl tablecloth would be good protection for the tabletop.
3. Tear newspaper into strips $3/4$" wide. Torn strips are better than cut strips because they blend in more easily.
4. Mix papier-mâché according to directions on box.
5. Dip strips in paste. Cover the bottle by wrapping strips around it, overlapping them about $1/4$". Smooth each strip from the middle outward to remove bubbles and excess paste. When you reach the bottom of the bottle, use short, vertical strips that curl under the bottom edge to cover it.
6. Gently twist several soaked strips of newspaper together to make a long, thick rope that can be used for the head or arms.
7. To make the head, wrap two or three ropes around the bottle pressing them down so that they adhere. Then wrap smooth dipped strips around the bumpy rope surface to even it out. Pinch out a tiny nose in the appropriate spot.

Step 6

Step 5

Step 7

SS3823

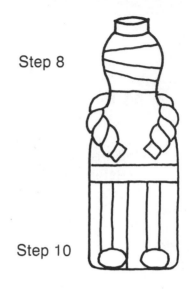

Step 8

8. For arms, bring a rope behind head and down both sides. Make hands with small wads of paper dipped in paste and placed at ends of arms.

9. You may also want to make a papier-mâché pulp at this time to aid in smoothing the surfaces. Make this pulp by tearing small pieces of newspaper and mixing them with a little water in a blender or food processor. Use this pulp to fill in crevices and holes on the surface of the bottle person.

Step 10

10. Add feet by wadding two small pieces of paper into small balls, dipping into paste, then placing at center on the bottom edge.

11. Be sure to let the papier-mâché dry thoroughly. This may take from two days to a week. The outside may feel dry, but if it feels cool, it probably is not dry on the under layers. Speed dry by using one of these three methods:
   a. Place in direct sunlight.
   b. Set near a radiator or under a heat lamp.
   c. Bake slowly in oven at 150°F with door propped open slightly. Check often to make sure paper is not charring.

Step 14

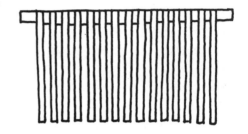

12. When the papier-mâché is dry, paint and decorate the bottle person.

13. Paint clothes and features first.

Step 15

14. To make hair, cut a narrow strip of paper that wraps around top of head. Glue short strips of yarn to paper. Glue this yarn-filled strip on top of head.

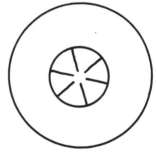

15. Make the hat by cutting a circle and slashing the center in the same way you would section a pie. Fit the hat on top of bottle and cover with a smaller circle to cover opening. Use a band of paper or ribbon to cover the cuts.

16. Be creative and add ribbon, buttons, flowers, etc.

BIBLICAL TEACHING:
What did you think about before you made your bottle person? Did you plan what he or she should look like? God planned people very carefully before He made them. Read about it in Genesis 1:26-27.

42

SS3823

Italy

PRESSED FLOWERS
Phun with phone books and phlowers!

In the early 1600s someone in Rome spread the good news about drying flowers and foliage to preserve some of their beauty. A very simple technique to use is pressing.

MATERIALS:
Flowers or interesting foliage
Phone book
Books or heavy objects

INSTRUCTIONS:
1. Select flowers or leaves to be pressed.
2. Separate the flowers or leaves as much as possible and place them between separate pages in the phone book.
3. Close the phone book and stack more books or heavy objects on the top to weight it down.
4. Drying time is two to four weeks, depending on the thickness of the foliage.
5. When dried, you can frame the flowers, use them to decorate note cards, or arrange them with pinecones and fall items for a simple centerpiece.

BIBLICAL TEACHING:
We press flowers because we want their beauty to last. God tells us that flowers fade away and die. However, His Word will last forever! Read Isaiah 40:8.

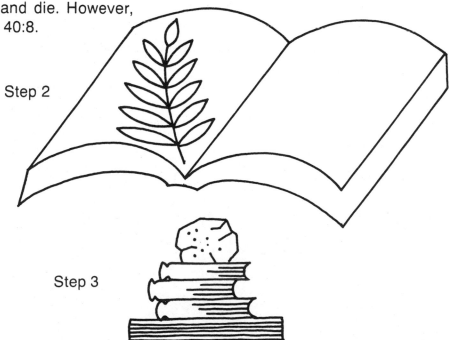

Step 2

Step 3

SS3823

Italy

PUNCH-AND-JUDY PUPPETS

Punch is the oldest and most famous puppet in Europe. His friend Judy joined him about 100 years later. Punch and Judy had lots of adventures on stage. You can make simple Punch-and-Judy puppets too.

MATERIALS:
Puppet and stage patterns (pages 45-46)
Markers
Light cardboard
Scissors
Glue
Straws

INSTRUCTIONS:
1. Cut out the puppets and stage, using the patterns on pages 45-46.
2. Use markers to add color and design.
3. Glue the puppets and stage to cardboard and trim.
4. Glue straws to the tabs as shown.
5. Cut slits in the stage.
6. Insert the puppets from the front into the stage so that the tabs are behind and project below.
7. Use the puppets to tell a story to a friend.

BIBLICAL TEACHING:
A puppet is not free to do what it wants. It can only do what you make it do. God gives us the freedom to make choices. He want us to serve Him, but He doesn't force us to. Read Joshua 24:14-15 to find out the choice the Israelites had to make.

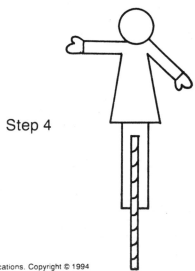

Step 4

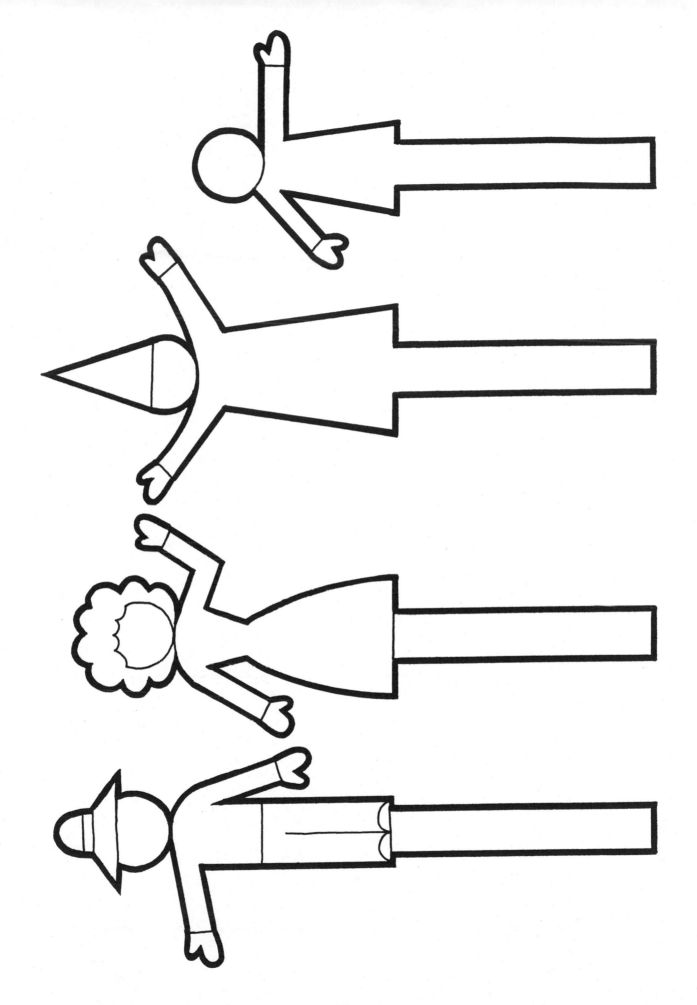

Shining Star Publications. Copyright © 1994

SS3823

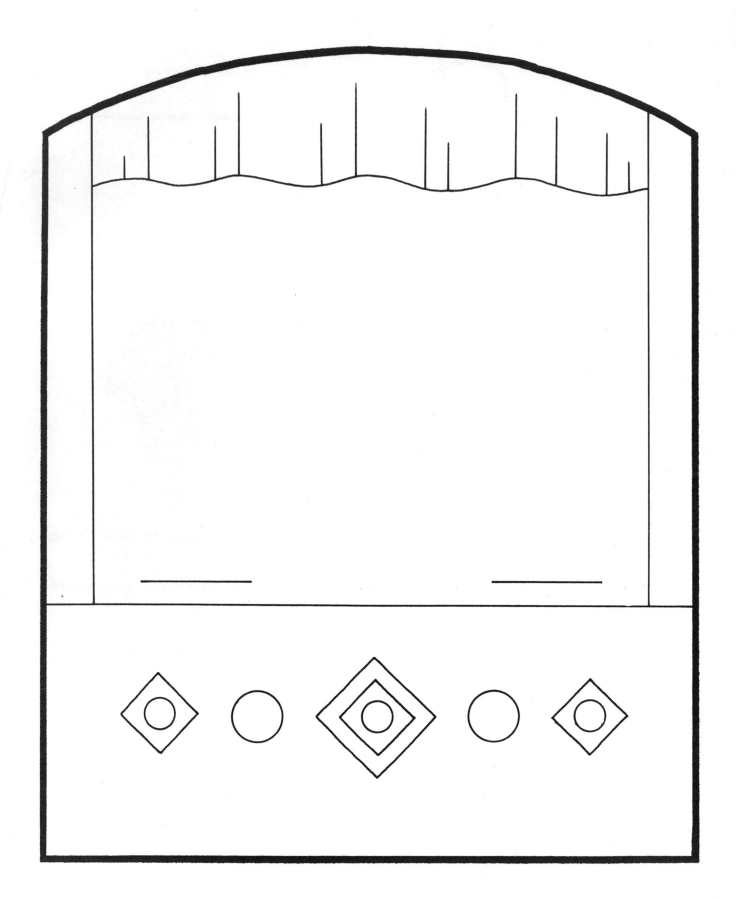

46

SS3823

Japan

RICE BAGS
Bags of rice to juggle are nice!

We often think of paper folding or origami when we think of Japan, but children there enjoy other activities too. One game especially enjoyed by girls is juggling. What do they juggle? Bags of rice, of course. You can easily make rice bags, but can you juggle them?

MATERIALS:
Pattern (page 48)
Fabric scraps
Marker
Scissors
Funnel
Rice or small dry beans
Thread and needle

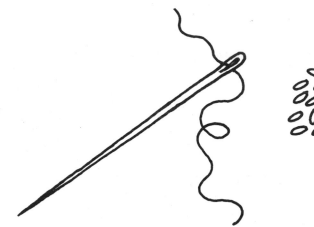

INSTRUCTIONS:
1. Cut out pattern on page 48 and trace two on fabric with a marker.
2. Cut out the fabric shapes.
3. Put right sides together.
4. If sewing, make very small stitches about $1/2$" from edge all the way around, leaving an opening of about 2".
5. Carefully turn right side out.
6. Use a funnel to fill the bag with rice.
7. Sew the opening very securely.
8. Practice your juggling or play catch.

Step 3

Step 4

Step 7

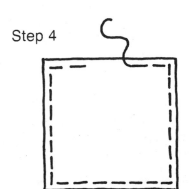

SS3823

VARIATION:
Use glue to seal the edges instead of sewing. Cut out the pattern with pinking shears instead of scissors. Put wrong sides together because you will have no need to turn it. Glue about 1/2" from the edge, leaving an opening for putting the rice. Glue must be thoroughly dry before stuffing or throwing the bag.

BIBLICAL TEACHING:
Sometimes Christians try to "juggle" serving God and doing their own thing. God says we have to be true to Him or true to our own desires. We can't do both! Read Matthew 6:24.

X Leave unsewn until turned. **X**

SS3823

Java

BATIK T-SHIRTS
Wax and cracks, color with dye, give it a try–it's batik!

Java, an island in the Republic of Indonesia, is filled with colorful creatures such as peacocks, jungle fowl, gorgeous fish, and over 500 species of butterflies. It is not surprising that batik, which features brilliant colors on cloth, is primarily called a Javanese art form. And it's fun!

MATERIALS:
Cotton T-shirt (prewashed to remove sizing)
16-oz. package of paraffin
Paintbrushes
Cardboard cut to fit inside shape of shirt
Colored fabric dye dissolved according to directions and cooled in a large pan or bucket
Rubber gloves
Newspapers
Paper towels
Iron

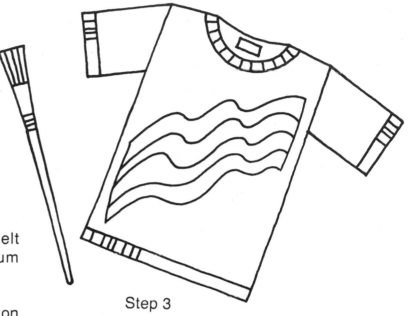

Step 3

INSTRUCTIONS:
1. ADULT SUPERVISION NEEDED: Melt paraffin in double boiler over medium heat.
2. Stretch shirt on piece of cardboard.
3. Dip brush into wax and make designs on the shirt. These designs will be white after your first dyeing.
4. When wax is dry on front of shirt, make designs on the back.
5. When back is dry remove from cardboard and immerse in dye. Wax will crumble as you press the shirt into the dye.

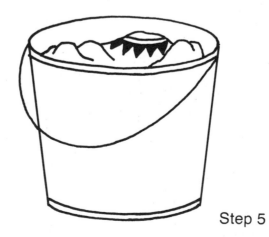

Step 5

6. Rinse in a clean container under cold running water until water is clear and no dye runs out. (Stains on sink can be cleaned with bleach.)

7. Hang the shirt to dry.

8. Because drying will take longer than a class session, start over at the next class time, doing steps 1-6 again. The wax you paint on will save the color of the first dye bath.

9. Repeat the process as many times as desired.

10. ADULT SUPERVISION NEEDED: When the shirt has dried for the last time, layer newspapers, paper towels, the shirt, paper towels, and a final layer of newspapers. Iron without steam to melt wax.

11. ADULT SUPERVISION NEEDED: Any leftover wax can be removed with lighter fluid.

12. Wash shirt in cold water hereafter because cool-dyeing does not make the colors fast.

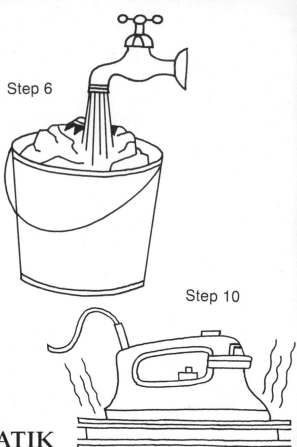

Step 6

Step 10

EASY CRAYON BATIK

MATERIALS:
White cotton T-shirt
Crayons
Newspapers
Paper towels
Iron

INSTRUCTIONS:
1. Draw bright picture on T-shirt.
2. Put newspapers inside shirt and paper toweling over design.
3. ADULT SUPERVISION NEEDED: Iron over design area. The wax will be absorbed, but the coloring in the crayon, the pigment, will stay on the fabric.
4. Change paper towels each time the color in the picture seems to be coming off and not just the wax. When it stops coming off, your shirt is finished.

Note: This method is quick but will fade when washed.

BIBLICAL TEACHING:
Does this shirt of many colors remind you of Joseph's coat of many colors? Read Genesis 37:3-4. Why did Joseph's brothers hate him?

STONE GAMES
Can you knock a rock out of a block? Sure!

A nationally enjoyed board game in Korea is played with black and white stones and is called paduk. We have some games that are similar that can also be played with black and white stones.

MATERIALS:
Patterns (pages 52-53)
6 dark-colored stones
6 light-colored stones
Scissors

INSTRUCTIONS:
1. Cut out the patterns on pages 52-53.
2. Give dark stones to one person and light stones to another.

TIC-TAC-TOE

Take turns placing your stones in the squares on the Tic-Tac-Toe pattern. The person who gets three stones in a row wins. If no one gets three stones in a row, the "cat" wins!

KNOCK THE ROCK

Place the Knock the Rock gameboard on the floor. Seat two players at least two feet from the board. Take turns tossing rocks onto the gameboard, trying to place them in the highest scoring sections. You may also try to knock the rock belonging to your opponent out of a high scoring section and put yours in. Toss the stones as if skipping rocks on water. After each person has tossed his rocks, count your points.

Note: If two rocks are in the 10-point section that would be 20. The person with the highest score is declared the winner.

VARIATION:
If you are unable to find rocks to use, make your own with bread, glue, and paint. Shred the insides of ten pieces of white bread. Add glue to make a soft dough. Form twelve round "stones" and let them dry overnight. Then paint six dark and six light. Homemade stones!

BIBLICAL TEACHING:
In the Bible, sinful people are said to have hearts of stone. But God says He loves us and wants to remove those stoney hearts. Read His promise in Ezekiel 36:26-27.

Tic-Tac-Toe

SS3823

Knock the Rock

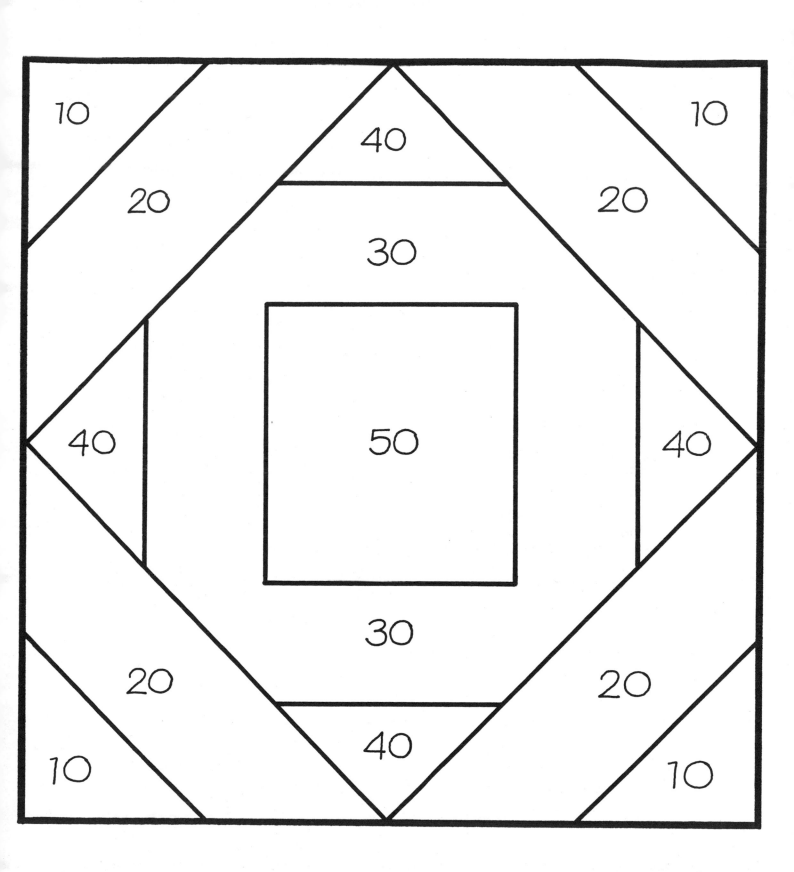

SS3823

ARCTIC SCENE

Lapland is a region north of the Arctic Circle which stretches across the top of Norway, Sweden, Finland, and the Commonwealth of Independent States. Laps used to primarily follow their reindeer herds and build temporary homes from branches and skins as they moved from place to place.

MATERIALS:
1 or 2 paper grocery bags
8 small straight branches about 8"-10" in length
Glue
Brown or black yarn
Aluminum foil
Cotton balls, batting, or stuffing
Patterns (pages 55-56)
Cardboard
Scissors
Pencil

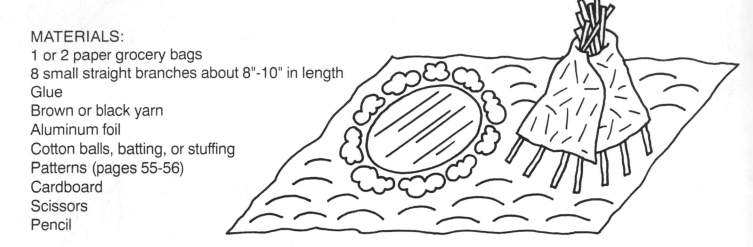

INSTRUCTIONS:
1. Cut a 12" x 12" piece from the grocery bag to serve as your base. Glue it to a piece of sturdy cardboard the same size.
2. Cut out reindeer skin, using the pattern on page 55.
3. Trace four or five skins on paper bags and cut out.
4. Wad them up, making wrinkles to soften, then smooth out again.
5. Cut out the circle pattern on page 56.
6. Trace a circle on aluminum foil. Glue down near a corner on the base paper to represent a pond.
7. Place wads of batting around the pond to look like snowdrifts.
8. Trace and cut out a circle from the paper bag.
9. Glue this circle down in the opposite corner and surround with wads of cotton batting.
10. Lay sticks in a pile with one end as even as possible (page 55).
11. Tie sticks together securely with a piece of yarn about 2" from the top (page 55).
12. Open bundle of sticks tepee fashion over paper bag circle with even bottoms resting in edge of the cotton batting (page 55).
13. Glue "skins" around tent poles, overlapping to make tepee, as shown.

Step 9

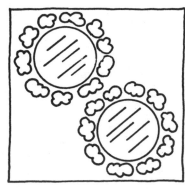

Step 10

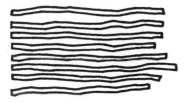

Steps 11-12

Reindeer Skin Pattern

Pond and Tent Bottom Pattern

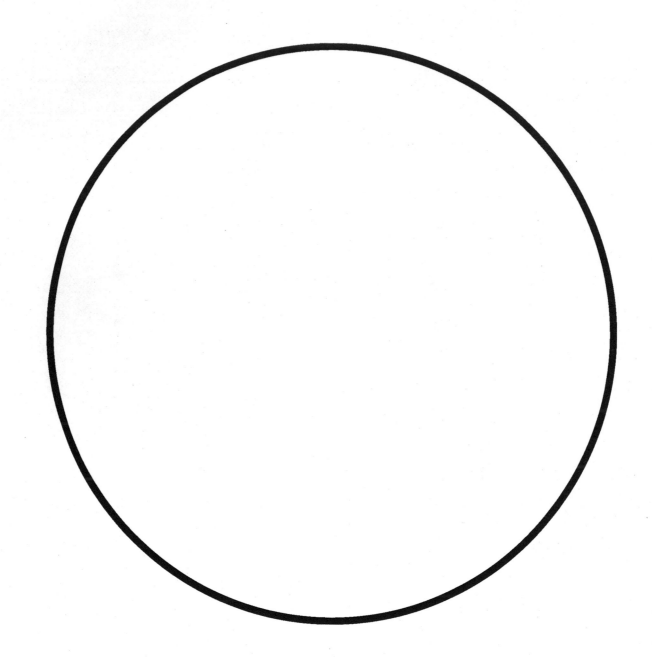

SS3823

Lithuania and the Ukraine
BATIK EGGS
"Eggs"traordinary!

In the early Christian church eggs were a central part in the Easter celebration. Lithuania and the Ukraine, once a part of the Commonwealth of Independent States, are famous for their beautifully decorated eggs. In Lithuania the technique is called margutis, and in the Ukraine it's pysanka. With a few simple household items you can practice your hand at similar eggs.

MATERIALS:
Eggs (blown, raw, or hard-boiled—hard-boiled may be the easiest for children to handle)
Wax (candle or beeswax)
Vinegar
Pencils with erasers
Straight pins (with various-sized heads)
Margarine tubs with water
Food coloring
Egg carton
Drawing paper
Tablespoon

Step 3

INSTRUCTIONS:
1. Use cold water to fill four margarine tubs three-fourths full.
2. Add 1 tablespoon of vinegar and three to four drops of food coloring to each. (You may want to make more than the four basic colors by mixing two colors together, such as red and yellow to make orange.)
3. Sketch your design out first on a piece of paper. (Drawing lines on the egg will show through wax and dye.)
4. Make wax markers by sticking straight pins with various-sized heads into pencil erasers.
5. ADULT SUPERVISION NEEDED: Melt wax over heat in a double boiler, never over a direct flame.
6. Dip wax marker tip into melted wax and draw design on egg. Apply wax to areas you don't want dyed. That's why this is called a wax-resistant method.

Step 4

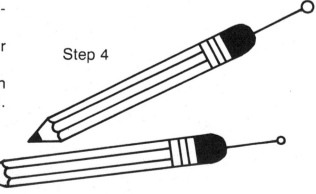

SS3823

7. When your design is done and the wax has cooled, dip egg in first dye bath. A white design will appear on places where you've used the wax marker. Start with the lightest dye, working toward the darkest (yellow, orange, red, green, blue, purple).
8. Draw more designs on the egg with the wax marker. When this is cooled, dip into the next color. You will have designs that are the color of the first dye bath.
9. Repeat this process as many times as you like. Remember, practice makes perfect—well, almost!

Note: Do not rub or pat dry or the dye will rub off.

HELPFUL HINT: Use an empty egg carton turned upside down with bottoms of cups sliced off to hold drying or finished eggs.

BIBLICAL TEACHING:
Did you know that God has promised to do a dye job on those who turn to Him? Read Isaiah 1:18.

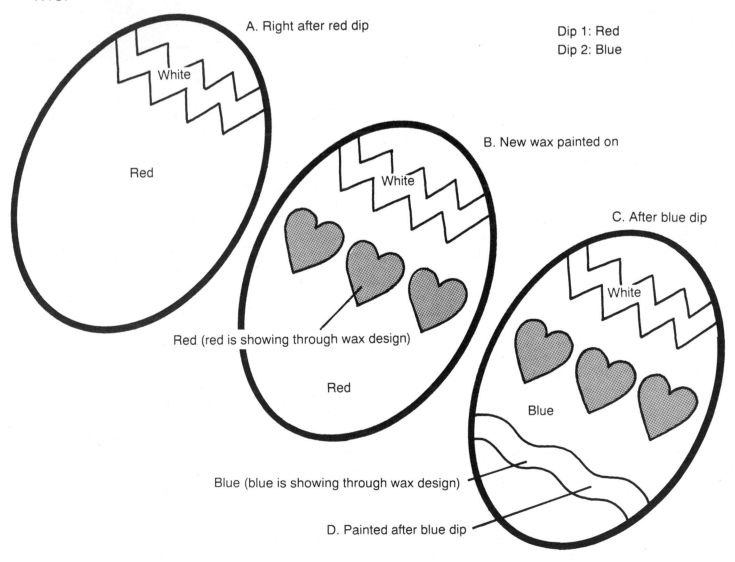

A. Right after red dip

White

Red

Dip 1: Red
Dip 2: Blue

B. New wax painted on

White

Red (red is showing through wax design)

Red

C. After blue dip

White

Blue

Blue (blue is showing through wax design)

D. Painted after blue dip

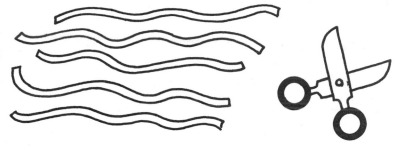

Mexico

RAG DOLLS
Dolls from scraps to hold on laps

If you visit Mexico on Christmas Eve, you may see rag dolls being held tightly by little children as they sit through special holiday services with their families. These dolls are easy to make.

MATERIALS:
30 strips of cloth about 16" long
6 small pieces of yarn or string about 5" long
Scissors
Ruler

INSTRUCTIONS:
1. Place strips of cloth in a pile matching ends as closely as possible.
2. Fold entire pile in half and tie a strip of yarn about 2" from top of fold to form a head.
3. Separate fifteen strips on either side and trim about 3". Tie a strip of yarn about 1" from ends to create hands.
4. To make a girl, tie a piece of yarn 2½" down from the head to form a waist. Spread out remaining strips for a skirt. For a boy, tie at waist but divide remaining strips into two equal legs with yarn tied about 1" from ends for feet.

VARIATIONS:
1. Use 12" pieces of yarn instead of cloth strips.
2. Tie strips with ribbon instead of yarn. Tie a ribbon at top of head also. Add a tiny piece of lace at waist for an apron.
3. Stick a dowel up into the doll and secure to make a puppet.

BIBLICAL TEACHING:
Our dolls are made from clean rags, but the Bible talks about "filthy" rags. God says our righteous acts are like filthy rags. That means our good deeds are worth nothing without faith in Him. Read about it in Isaiah 64:6.

Step 1

SS3823

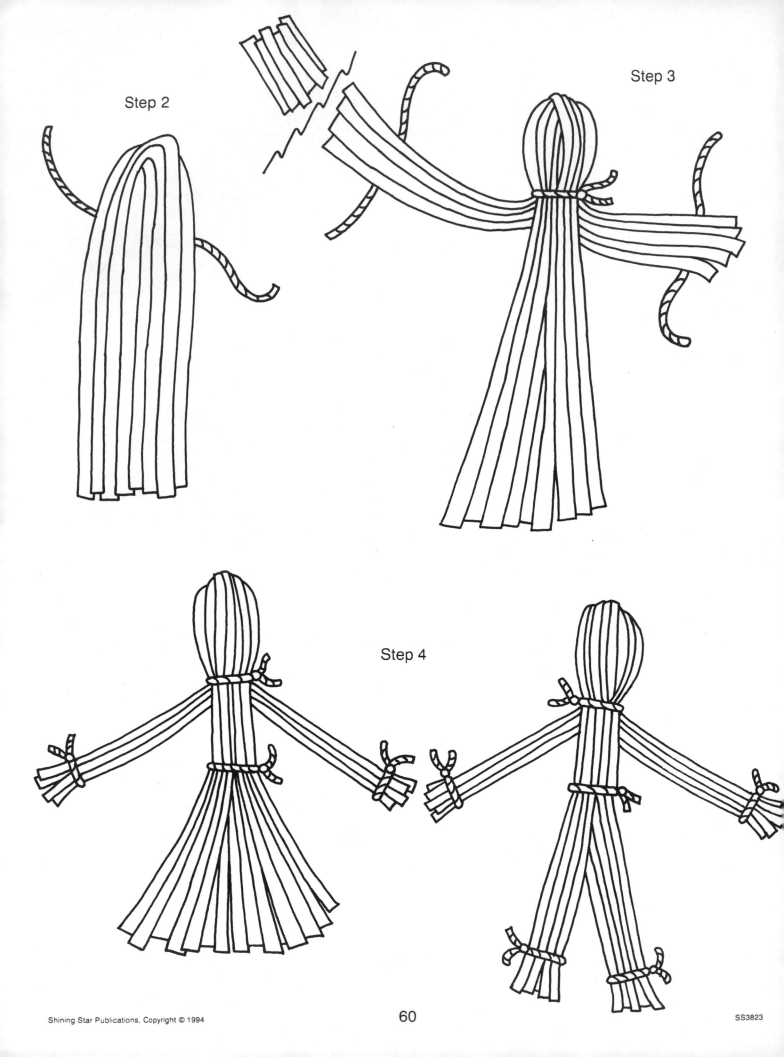

Step 2

Step 3

Step 4

SS3823

ANIMATED BOOKS
A book without words for all ages!

Nepal is a beautiful country located astride the Himalaya Mountains. It's a very popular spot for tourists. Only about one-third of its people can read, so artwork called thangka, colorful pictures on fabric which tell a story, is widespread. Use a group of pictures like thangka to make a story without words, but give yours movement.

MATERIALS:
Patterns (page 61-62)
Scissors
Stapler
Markers or crayons

INSTRUCTIONS:
1. Cut out the patterns on pages 61-62 and assemble in order, folding on the broken lines with the blank side folded behind the picture.
2. Color the figures, using the same colors for the same objects in each picture.
3. Staple at the left, unfolded edges in two or three spots.
4. Hold the book with one hand, flip the pages with the other, and watch the people move!
5. Make up your own story without words!

BIBLICAL TEACHING:
The Bible is God's book. What is the main message in His book? Read Jeremiah 31:3.

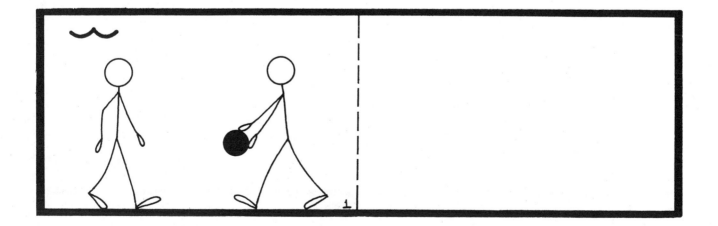

Cut on dark lines.

SS3823

Netherlands

PINWHEELS

The Netherlands is a country about the size of Massachusetts, Connecticut, and Rhode Island combined. Traditionally one thinks of dikes, Hans Brinker's silver skates, and windmills when thinking of this country. Just see how easy windmills or pinwheels are to make.

MATERIALS:
Pattern (bottom of this page)
Pencil with eraser
Straight pin
Markers or crayons
Scissors

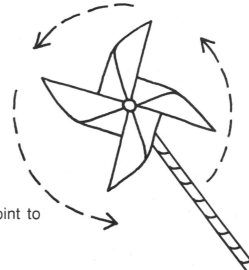

INSTRUCTIONS:
1. Color and cut out the pattern below.
2. Cut on the diagonal lines.
3. Bring all corners with dots together and attach this point to pencil erasers with a straight pin.
4. Blow on your pinwheel and watch it spin.

BIBLICAL TEACHING:
Do you ever feel like you're going around in circles like the pinwheel? Do you have too much to do? Do you have trouble making choices? Read Proverbs 3:5-6; then ask God to direct you.

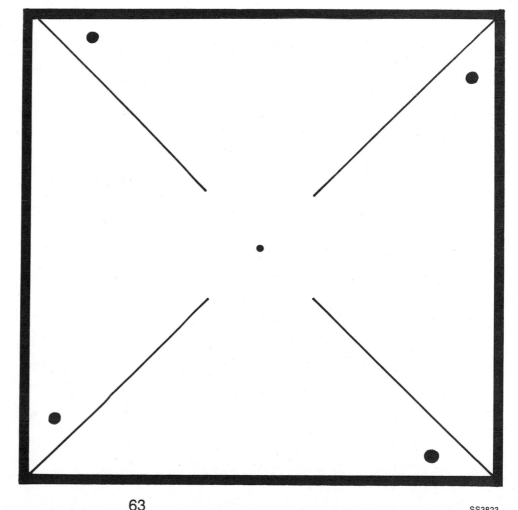

SS3823

BEADS

Beautiful beads are hiding in the kitchen and the living room!

Tribal jewelry in various parts of the world can show that you are married, unmarried, happy, sad, a good hunter, grown-up, peaceful, or on the warpath. Here are some ways to make jewelry to match your mood.

BREAD BEADS

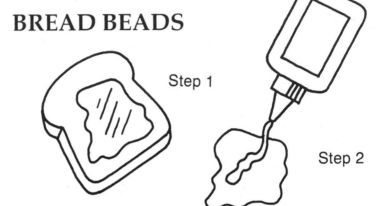

MATERIALS:
10 slices of white bread
Knife
Glue
Toothpicks
Acrylic paints
Paintbrush

INSTRUCTIONS:
1. Cut off the crusts of ten slices of white bread.
2. Mix with glue to form soft dough.
3. Shape into round and square beads.
4. Poke holes with toothpicks and dry overnight.
5. Paint with acrylics.

STYROFOAM™ AND STRAW BEADS

MATERIALS:
Colored Styrofoam™ trays
Straws
Scissors
Hole punch
String or shoelace

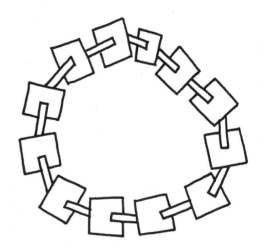

INSTRUCTIONS:
1. Cut Styrofoam™ trays into 1" circles and squares. Punch a hole in each center.
2. Cut straws into ¹/₂" lengths.
3. String together, alternating a Styrofoam™ shape with a section of straw.

SS3823

ROLL-UP BEADS

MATERIALS:
Pattern on this page
Newspaper or magazine pictures
Scissors
Straws
Glue
Clear nail polish
Pencil

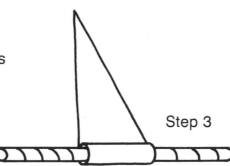

Step 3

INSTRUCTIONS:
1. Cut out triangle pattern on this page.
2. Trace the pattern on colorful paper and cut out.
3. Wrap triangle around end of straw, starting with wide end.
4. Glue pointed tip down when rolling is completed.
5. Cut off ends of straw leaving straw section inside.
6. When glue is dry, coat with clear nail polish for shiny finish.

Step 5

EDIBLE BEADS

MATERIALS:
Candy corn
Orange slice candy
LifeSavers™
Froot Loops™
Containers
Needle
Yarn or string

INSTRUCTIONS:
Gather your edible materials and separate into containers. You will need a needle with a point for the candy corn and orange slices.

STRINGING BEADS:
1. Use yarn or string on a large-eyed needle for stringing the edible beads. Plastic needles may work for some of the materials.
2. Tie a LifeSaver™ or a bead at the end of the string instead of a knot, which is sometimes too small.
3. Use 36" of string for necklace and 14" for a wrist or ankle bracelet.

BIBLICAL TEACHING:
God's Word tells us about a special way He wants to dress us up! Read Isaiah 61:10.

Norway

ROSEMALING
A flower, a leaf, and other motifs–that's rosemaling!

Rosemaling was popular for interior decorating in Norway from 1700 to 1850. It was used on furniture, walls, ceiling, and doors. The colors are limited mostly to reds, blues, greens, and yellow with accents in off-white and black. One style was developed in the Hallingdal district and was very symmetrical. That's the style we'll try!

MATERIALS:
Patterns (page 67)
Markers
Sponges
Water
Sharp scissors
Paint (tempera, acrylic, or homemade in same colors as
  construction paper)
Margarine tubs
Construction paper (red, blue, yellow, green, or black)
Plain paper

FOLDED ROSEMALING PICTURE

INSTRUCTIONS:
1. Cut out patterns. Use markers to trace patterns on sponges.
2. Cut out.
3. Put paint into margarine tubs.
4. Fold paper in half, unfold.
5. Moisten sponge pieces with water. (They should not be drippy.)
6. Dip damp sponges in paint and stamp shapes on half of the folded paper as shown.
7. When you finish the design, fold paper in half again on original fold line and press together. A copy of your design will be imprinted on the other side of the paper.

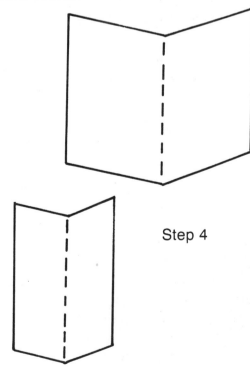

Step 4

Step 6

Step 7

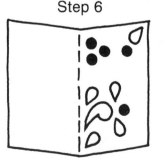

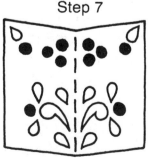

ROSEMALING NAME POSTERS

INSTRUCTIONS:
1. Follow steps 1, 2, and 3 on previous project.
2. Use sponges to make rosemaling shapes around edge of paper.
3. Write your name in the middle.

HOMEMADE PAINT

INSTRUCTIONS:
1. Mix equal amounts, about a cup each, of flour and salt.
2. Mix with water until the consistency of tempera paint.
3. Divide into two or three margarine tubs, adding different food coloring to each.

Note: This paint dries at a lighter shade than its original color. It should be used only on white or light yellow paper. The salt makes it textured and sometimes a little glittery.

BIBLICAL TEACHING:

If you want your rosemaling to be good, you need to carefully follow the instructions. Are you also careful to follow God's instructions for your life? Read Psalm 32:8.

Sponge Patterns

SS3823

Pakistan

MOSAIC
Bits and pieces, pieces and bits, just make sure everything fits!

A mosaic is a fragmented design in which many pieces are fitted together to make a complete picture. Mosaic pebble floors done in artistic patterns dating from 7000 B.C. have been found in caves. Today beautiful mosaic walls and art can be found in many Asian countries including Pakistan. A mosaic can be created with almost any collection of small, easily glued items. Try it!

MATERIALS:
Cardboard
Construction paper
Glue
Plastic margarine tubs
Paintbrushes or cotton swabs
Pencil
Small easy-to-glue objects (buttons, pebbles, shells, pasta, hard candy, cereals, beans, seeds, hardware nuts and washers, beads, bottle caps, eggshells, fabric scraps, or paper)

SS3823

INSTRUCTIONS:

1. Divide the objects by color and/or shape in margarine tubs (or in egg cartons or muffin tins).
2. Show mosaic samples. Mosaics can be compared to making puzzles.
3. On a piece of construction paper draw simple, bold shapes such as fruit, a vegetable, animal, or face. A rainbow is a great mosaic project. (A picture with too much detail can be frustrating for young artists.)
4. Glue picture carefully on piece of cardboard and let dry. (Using colorful tagboard can eliminate this gluing step as it is bright and heavy enough to hold project.)
5. Use margarine tubs for holding glue.
6. Use brushes or cotton swabs for spreading glue on one section of the picture at a time.
7. Glue small objects one by one to picture.

ADDITIONAL IDEAS:

1. To encourage cooperation, create a group project where everyone works together on one large mural mosaic.
2. Mosaic art can also be used for decorating boxes, bottles, and cans for simple gifts.

BIBLICAL TEACHING:

When a mosaic is being worked on, it's hard to see any design in it. Only when it is completed, do we see how all the pieces fit together to make a beautiful picture. God works in us, fitting together all the tiny pieces of our lives to help us become what we should be. Read Romans 8:28.

SS3823

Panama

COVERED BOXES
Some metal, some lines, reflections shine!

Hundreds of years ago the Cocle Indians of Panama used specially made tools to hammer sheets of gold into beautiful works of art. Using aluminum foil and tools, you can try it too!

ORNAMENTAL BOX

MATERIALS:
Aluminum foil
Paper towels or napkins
Dull pencils
Glue or tape
Scissors
Small box with removable lid
White paper

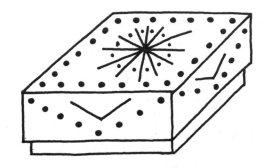

INSTRUCTIONS:
1. Measure around lid. Allow extra for flaps to go down sides and tuck under. Draw a pattern on a piece of paper.
2. Use pattern to make a double layer of paper toweling and aluminum foil.
3. Center paper towel on box top and glue to underside of lid.
4. Attach aluminum foil in same way, keeping it as smooth as possible and covering corners.
5. Use dull pencil to softly mark a design on top and sides of lid.
6. Cover bottom of box, using steps 1-4 above. Add designs.
7. Cover box with lid.

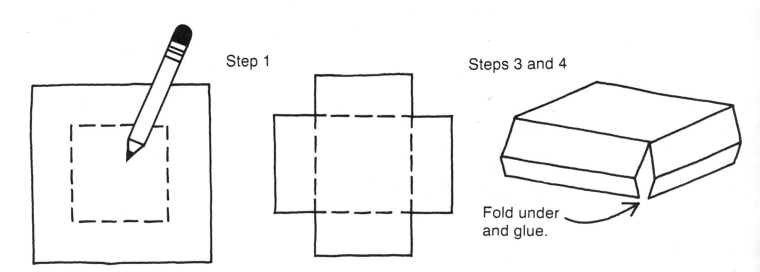

Step 1

Steps 3 and 4

Fold under and glue.

SS3823

ORNAMENTAL PICTURE FRAME

MATERIALS:
Disposable cake pan or cookie sheet of heavy aluminum
Dull pencil
Metal fork
Small heart-shaped cookie cutter
Utility scissors
Colored tape

INSTRUCTIONS:
1. Decide on size of frame you desire. Draw frame with pencil on aluminum and cut out.
2. Use fork to make dots all around the edges.
3. Press hearts at corners, outlining with dots.
4. Fold colored tape around frame to cover sharp edges.

BIBLICAL TEACHING:
Gold and silver have always been treasured by people and used for special decorations and jewelry. King David gave gold and silver and other expensive gifts for God's temple. Read about it in 1 Chronicles 29:1-5. Why do you think David donated these to the temple?

SS3823

Peru

JEWELRY
Jewelry of gold to have and to hold!

The Inca Indians of Peru made gold jewelry as early as 300 B.C. Use some materials that shine like gold to make your own jewelry.

MATERIALS:
Black construction paper
Scissors
Glue
Margarine tubs
Cotton swabs
Gold and silver glitter
Sequins
Aluminum foil
Yarn or paper clips
Hole punch
Tape

INSTRUCTIONS:
1. Cut black paper circles, squares, and diamonds. You may want to find cups and other objects to trace.
2. Punch a hole at the top of each piece.
3. Use margarine tubs for holding glue.
4. Decorate by gluing on glitter or sequins. Use cotton swabs for spreading glue.
5. Use aluminum foil to make some shapes, also punching holes at the top.
6. Use yarn or paper clip chains for hanging your "medallions"!
7. Aluminum foil may also be used for making silver bracelets or headbands. Roll a strip and tape it in a circle.
8. Be creative!

BIBLICAL TEACHING:
Gold is worth a lot, but there's something that's worth more. Read Psalm 119:72 to see what it is. Do you agree with the writer of the Psalm?

Shining Star Publications. Copyright © 1994

SS3823

Philippines

WEAVINGS
Do you believe that you can weave? I do!

The Philippines is a country of 7100 islands. Two of the main industries are textiles and clothing, so it is not a surprise that weaving is done by many of the Filipinos. They use bright colors. Let's do the same as we try our hand at weaving.

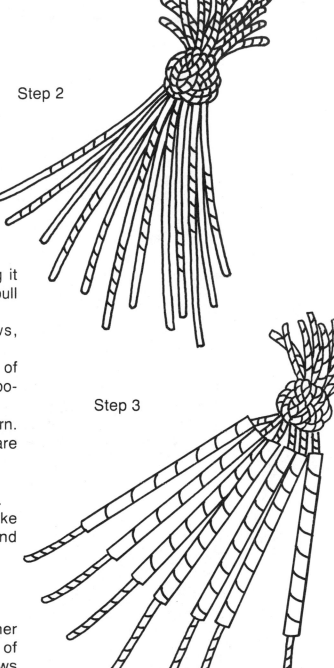

Step 2

Step 3

MATERIALS:
Bright-colored yarn
Straws
Small paper clip
Metal hairpins
Scissors
Tape
Ruler

INSTRUCTIONS:
1. Cut eight 24" pieces of variously colored yarn.
2. Knot the pieces of yarn together.
3. Lace each piece of yarn through a straw, taping it loosely to the end of the straw. Use a hairpin to pull the yarn through the straw.
4. When all the yarn is laced through the straws, remove tape and tie yarn in another knot.
5. Use a paper clip as a "shuttle." Tie a long piece of yarn to it, and weave it over the straws. Do the opposite on the next row.
6. When adding a new color, tie to end of previous yarn. These knots can be poked undercover when you are finished.
7. Weave until you have the straws almost full.
8. Untie one of the end knots and slide out the straws.
9. Leave your woven piece with the large knots or make a small fringe by tying the loose yarn in pairs and trimming shorter.

BIBLICAL TEACHING:
Many strands of many colors and kinds joined together make the most pleasing weavings. When Christians of many kinds join together, God is pleased. Read Hebrews 10:24-25.

Step 5

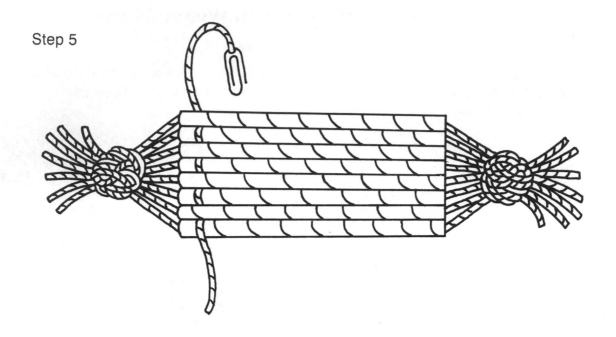

Step 9

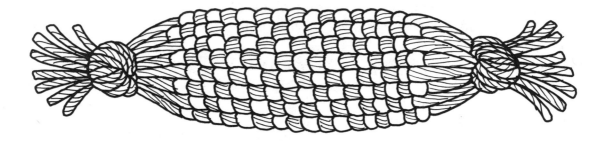

Poland

PAPER CUTTING
Intricate cutting with an eye for detail makes a lovely design.

Polish peasants often decorated their homes with paper patterns and designs which they pasted to their walls. These paper creations were called wycinanki and have become a traditional Polish folk art.

MATERIALS:
Pattern (page 76)
Black and white paper
Scissors
Glue
Pencil

INSTRUCTIONS:
1. Cut out pattern and trace onto a piece of paper which you have folded in half.
2. Cut out and open fold.
3. If done on white, glue onto black paper and vice versa.
4. Try your own design. Be creative and make it as tiny as you are able to cut around!

Note: These creations are beautiful for greeting cards.

BIBLICAL TEACHING:
A pattern is to be imitated. Christians should imitate God in all that they say and do. Read Ephesians 5:1.

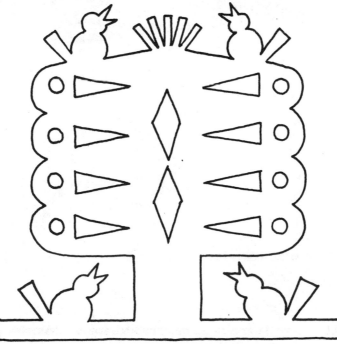

SS3823

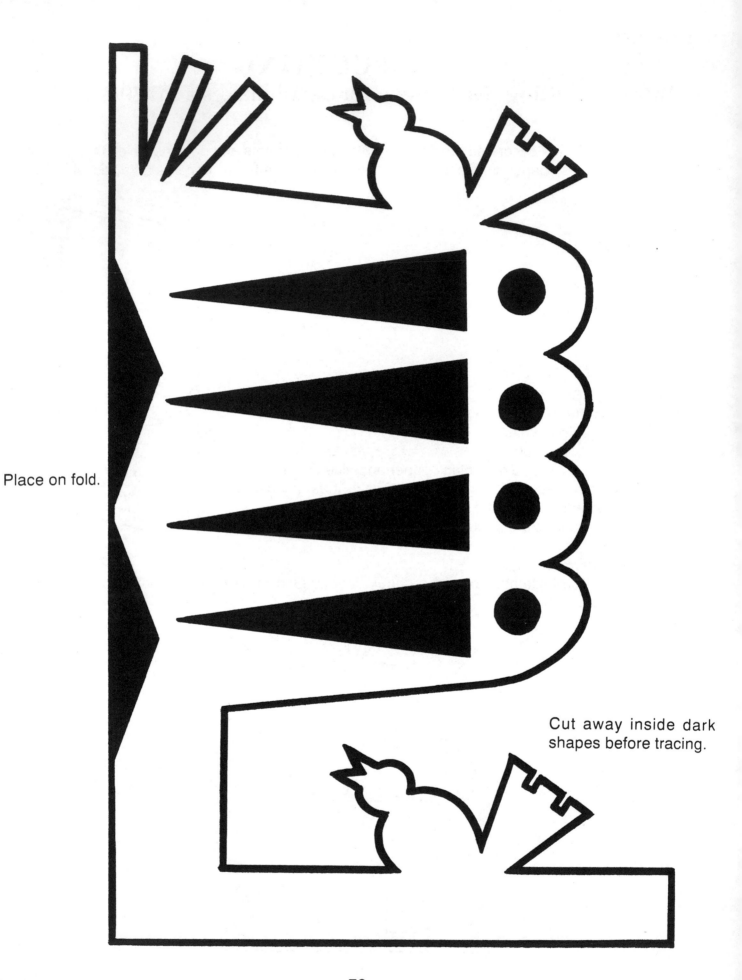

Place on fold.

Cut away inside dark shapes before tracing.

Poland

CARVING
And you thought carving was just for turkeys and wood!

In Poland a very special kind of art can be observed in a unique setting. Beautiful salt sculptures are found in salt mines near Kraków. Soap can be carved in a similar fashion.

MATERIALS:
Bar of soap (square bar without design or imprint on either side)
Pencil or pen
Plastic knife or dull kitchen knife

INSTRUCTIONS:
1. Draw a simple shape on soap, such as fish or flower, with design coming to edges as much as possible.
2. Carve away unnecessary soap.

OTHER IDEA:
If a boat shape is carved from a floating soap bar and a sail is added with a paper flag on a straw or toothpick, it makes a good toy for the bathtub.

BIBLICAL TEACHING:
Did you know that God punished Old Testament carvers? They carved idols for people to worship, and that was against God's law. Read Deuteronomy 27:15.

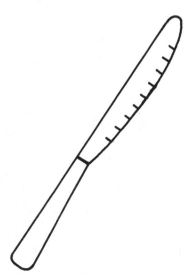
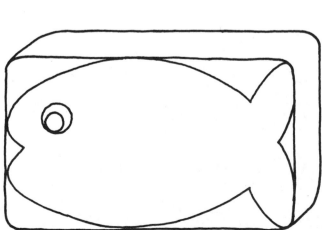
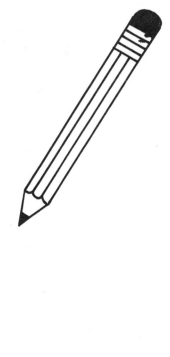

SS3823

Portugal

TILES
Decorating tiles for fun and smiles!

Portuguese artisans use colorful tiles inside and outside buildings. The tiles often display the geometric patterns and bright colors of the Moors who ruled Portugal beginning in the 700s. Tiles can be used for lots of neat projects.

TILE BOX

MATERIALS:
Tiles (ceramic or vinyl are available at hardware or flooring stores)
Permanent markers or acrylic paint
Glue
Cereal box cardboard

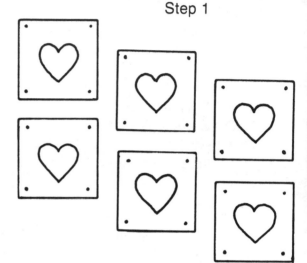

Step 1

INSTRUCTIONS:
1. Decorate six tiles so that they match each other in color and style.
2. Cut five strips of cardboard, each 3" wide and as tall as one of your tiles. Fold each strip in half lengthwise.
3. Glue two tiles at right angles against one laying flat.
4. Glue a cardboard strip in the corner as a brace.
5. Add a tile as a third wall, with another cardboard brace at the corner.
6. Repeat with the fourth wall, adding two braces.
7. Make extra braces for the bottom horizontal corners.
8. The sixth tile may be used for a loose lid, or you may want to use a brace as a hinge at the top of one of the tile walls.

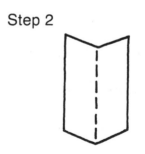

Step 2

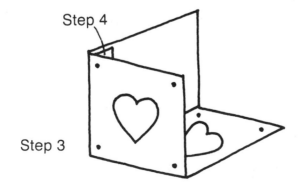

Step 4

Step 3

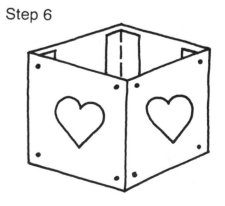

Step 6

TILE WELCOME MAT

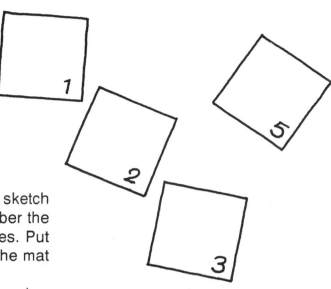

MATERIALS:
Tiles
Permanent markers
Large piece of cardboard (approximately 2' x 3')
Glue
Pencils

INSTRUCTIONS:
Decorate tiles in one of three ways:
1. Put tiles all in place on the cardboard mat and sketch a picture that stretches over all the tiles. Number the backs of the tiles; then have children color tiles. Put the tiles back together to form the picture on the mat and glue in place.
2. Color tiles with individual pictures; then glue to mat.
3. Come up with your own design.

VARIATION:
Instead of buying tiles, cut "tiles" from tagboard or cardboard.

BIBLICAL TEACHING:
When you work with your hands to make something, are you proud of it? Do you want to take care of it so that no harm comes to it? God made us, and now He takes care of us. Read Ephesians 2:10.

SS3823

Saudi Arabia

WEAVINGS
Bedouins camp inside a work of art! Can you eat on one?

The Bedouins of Saudi Arabia are nomads who travel from place to place with no permanent dwelling. Their homes are often tents made of beautifully woven tapestry. You can make a place mat that looks a little like their colorful works of art.

MATERIALS:
Pattern (page 81)
Cardboard from cereal box or gift box
Glue
Margarine tubs
Cotton swabs
Scissors
20" strips of colored yarn

Note: The diamond in center leaves no fringe.

INSTRUCTIONS:
1. Put glue into margarine tubs.
2. Glue pattern on page 81 on cardboard.
3. Use cotton swab to make a line of glue along edge of a geometric shape on pattern.
4. Lay yarn strip on glue line, leaving equal amount of yarn hanging over each side (approximately 5").
5. Repeat until pattern is filled.
6. When glue is dry, gather three or four strands of yarn hanging over edge and tie in small knots.

VARIATION:
Let the fringe hang over on one side only for tying knots. Roll mat into a tube. Glue or staple edges. Attach a string for hanging at the top and you have a "wind sock."

BIBLICAL TEACHING:
Did you know that the tabernacle that God told the Israelites to make was a tent? They packed it up and carried it with them wherever they went. That tent was their place to meet God. Read Exodus 40:1-3, 34-38.

SS3823

SS3823

Scotland

THISTLES
Saved by a thistle

The thistle became an important Scottish symbol in the early 1200s when an attacking Norwegian soldier stepped on its prickly leaves, yelling out in pain. His cry alerted the Scots to the enemy's position and helped them win the battle. Here's a way to make a thistle plant.

MATERIALS:
Purple or lavender yarn
1 envelope (approximately 3" x 6")
Green chenille stems
Green felt
Glue
Scissors
Leaf pattern (page 83)

Step 1

INSTRUCTIONS:
1. Fold envelope in half.
2. Wrap yarn around the envelope twenty-five times.
3. Tie at one edge with small piece of yarn.
4. Cut at the other edge and fluff.
5. Cut out felt leaves, using pattern on page 83.
6. Glue a folded chenille stem to the back of each leaf, leaving half of it hanging over the end for securing to the main stem.
7. Twist two chenille stems together for the main stem, making a round ledge at the top.
8. Glue the bottom of the yarn flower to the ledge.

BIBLICAL TEACHING:
Apparently before Adam and Eve sinned there were no thorns or thistles! Everything was truly perfect, but their sin ruined it. Read Genesis 3:17-19.

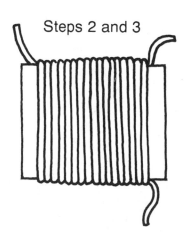

Steps 2 and 3

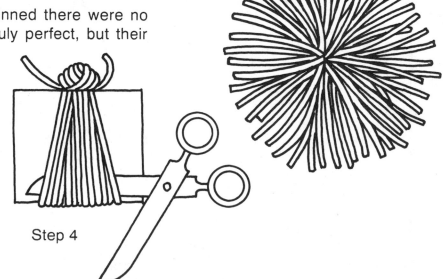

Step 4

SS3823

Leaf Pattern

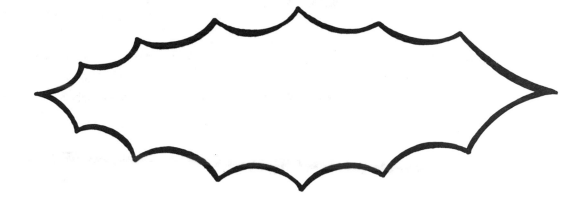

Step 6

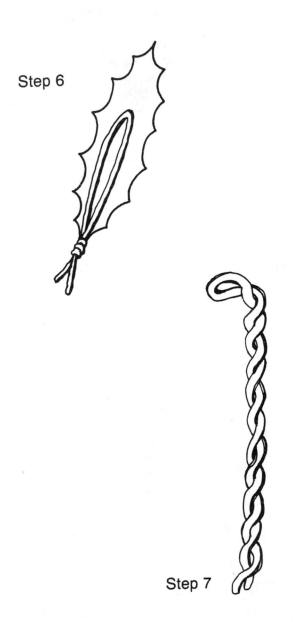

Step 7

Step 8

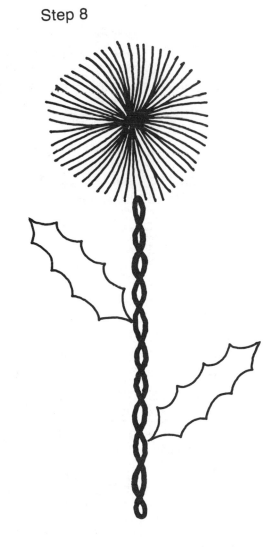

SS3823

PEACE PAINT

Throughout the history of South America, North America, and Africa there have been tribes at war with each other. Often war paint was a part of the preparation before setting off for battle. The opposite of war is peace. That's what you can enjoy because of Jesus! Let's make some peace paint!

EASY PEACE PAINT

MATERIALS:
Heavy cold cream
Food coloring
Margarine tubs
Spoons

INSTRUCTIONS:
1. Divide the cold cream into four margarine tubs.
2. Add a few drops of food coloring to each and stir. To make darker, add more food coloring.
3. Put on peace paint with your fingers, avoiding your eyes.

BIBLICAL TEACHING:
God wants His children to make peace, not war, with everyone. Read Matthew 5:9. How can we be peacemakers?

SS3823

South and Central America

BASKETS
A tisket, a tasket, let's make a basket!

Basket-making is not only one of man's oldest crafts, but one found all around the world. Basketry preceded pottery as a craft in the Americas dating back probably 9000 years. You can make a small basket that is just right for holding pencils, markers, or crayons.

MATERIALS:
1- or 2-liter plastic bottle
Scissors
Yarn (various colors)
Glue

INSTRUCTIONS:
1. Cut the "neck and shoulders" from the top of bottle.
2. Cut strips about 1" wide, down to plastic base. You will end up with thirteen to twenty strips.
3. Weave yarn in and out (over and under) strips, starting with end inside bottle.
4. Choose another color and keep weaving. Always leave ends inside. Repeat.
5. With scissors, round off plastic strip ends about 1" above last row of weaving.
6. Tuck ends of yarn into nearest weaving row and seal with drop of glue.

Step 1

BIBLICAL TEACHING:
Isn't it fun to take a throwaway item that seems useless and change it into something wonderful? That's what God does for people! Read Ephesians 2:1-5.

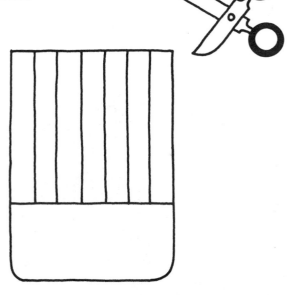

Step 2

SS3823

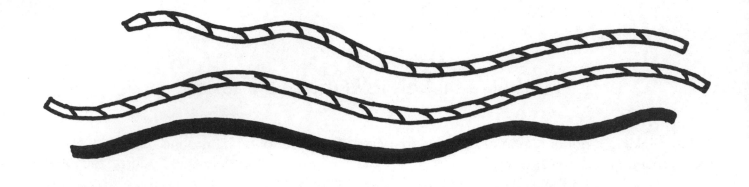

Step 3

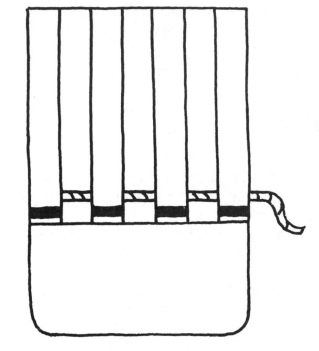

Step 4

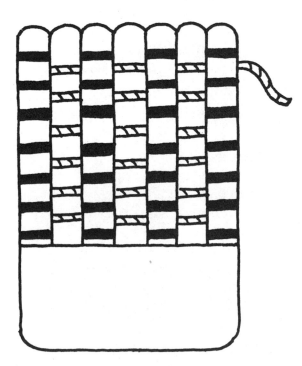

Step 5

Spain and Mexico

PIÑATA
Be sure to break this toy! A piñata!

Roman vineyard workers made early piñatas from clay pots and smashed them to mark the end of the harvest season. Caesar's troops took the idea to Spain, where it spread in later years to Mexico. Piñatas, teeming with surprises and treats, are still used today in both of these Spanish-speaking countries. Here are two ideas for making your own special piñatas.

FACE PIÑATA

MATERIALS:
Large balloon
Strips of newspaper torn in 1" wide strips
Liquid starch
Pink and black tissue paper
Glue
Buttons
Scissors
Yarn or string
Candy and/or other small treats
Pencil
Bat or broom

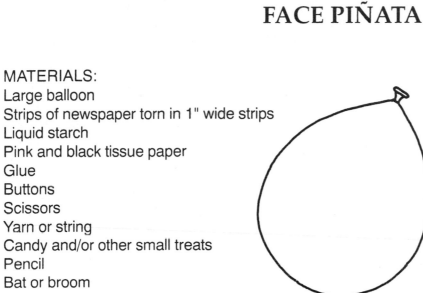

Step 1

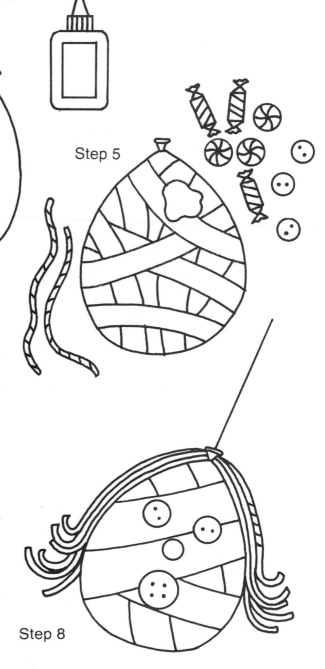

Step 5

Step 8

INSTRUCTIONS:
1. Blow up balloon and tie closed.
2. Dip strips of paper in liquid starch, pulling strips through your fingers to remove excess starch.
3. Cover balloon completely with paper over entire area. Leave top of balloon out where it has been tied. This will be used to tie a string for hanging.
4. Let it dry thoroughly.
5. Make small hole near top and fill with treats.
6. Cut pink tissue paper in strips about 4" wide, gluing them over the newspaper as you wrap.
7. Cut narrow strips of black. Glue them over the top for hair. Curl them by rolling strips tightly around pencil before adding to head.
8. Add buttons for nose, eyes, and mouth.
9. When dry, hang in a tree above head and allow blindfolded kids to break with a bat or broom.

Shining Star Publications. Copyright © 1994

SS3823

EASY GIFT BOX PIÑATA

MATERIALS:
Empty facial tissue box
Tissue paper
Ribbon
Glue
Candy and/or small treats
Yarn or string
Scissors
Bat or broom

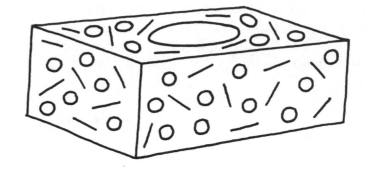

Step 1

INSTRUCTIONS:
1. Poke holes in the tissue box to weaken its sides for later breaking.
2. Fill it with treats.
3. Wrap it with tissue paper, using glue to secure paper to box.
4. Tie ribbon around box so a loop (of yarn, ribbon, or string) can be attached securely for hanging.
5. Hang the piñata and break it!

BIBLICAL TEACHING:
The piñata is best when it's broken. That's the way God wants our spirits to be–broken and humble–so that we will be open to Him, willing to accept whatever He has for us. Read Psalm 51:15-17.

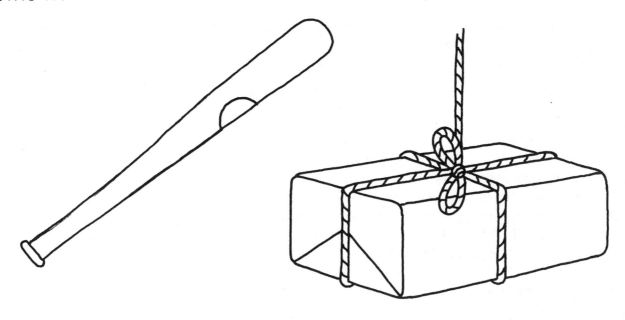

SS3823

Spain

SILHOUETTES
Fun shadows are really silhouettes!

Silhouettes are probably the oldest graphic art form. Silhouettes of animals and humans have been found in limestone caves in Spain. They may have been drawn over 20,000 years ago. Shadows are still around today, and so are silhouettes. Let's try two shadow craft projects.

EASY SIDEWALK SILHOUETTE

MATERIALS:
Chalk
Sunshine
Sidewalk or driveway
Water (for erasing if needed)
Friend or stable object

INSTRUCTIONS:
Have a friend stand in the sunlight to make a shadow that you can trace with your chalk. If there are no friends around, use your creativity and find some objects that won't move as you draw—a chair, a bike, a potted flower, etc.

WINDOW SILHOUETTE

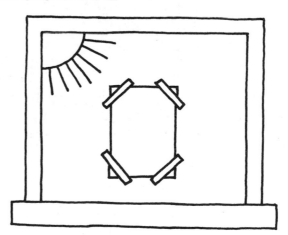

MATERIALS:
Typing paper
Pencil
Tape
Window
Friend
Sunshine

INSTRUCTIONS:
1. On a sunny day tape a piece of paper on a low window.
2. When the sun is shining directly in the window, have your friend stand so that his or her shadow falls on the paper.
3. Trace your friend's silhouette.
4. Optional: Finish the project by cutting around the silhouette and tracing it on black paper. Cut it out and glue on white paper.

BIBLICAL TEACHING:
God's Word tells us that we can rest in His shadow. You have to be very close to someone to stand in his shadow. Are you that close to God? Read Psalm 91:1.

SS3823

Sri Lanka

SANDALS
Sandals? Can your feet handle it?

In Sri Lanka, an island in the Indian Ocean off the southeast coast of India, the production of local crafts is encouraged by the government. One of its many crafts is sandals. These sandals may not last as long or be as detailed, but give them a try!

MATERIALS:
Pattern (page 91)
Tablecloth (vinyl)
Scissors
2 large buttons
Needle and thread
Pen or marker
Cardboard
Glue
Soft piece of cloth

Step 2

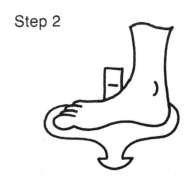

Step 3

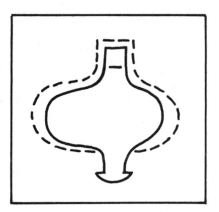

INSTRUCTIONS:
1. Cut out pattern on page 91.
2. Put your foot on the pattern. Decide if you need to adjust it by making it bigger or smaller. If adjustment is needed, make a new pattern.
3. Cut out pattern and trace with marker on vinyl.
4. Cut out and cut slit.
5. Sew on toe button, leaving it loose enough to fit your toe underneath.
6. Start on other foot, cutting out so the strap pulls across the opposite direction.
7. For padding, cut out a piece of cardboard to fit sandal pattern. Glue cardboard on a soft piece of cloth; then glue on your sandal.

BIBLICAL TEACHING:
In Old Testament days a legal transaction was finalized by one person taking off his sandal and giving it to the other! Read Ruth 4:7.

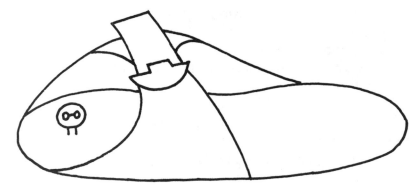

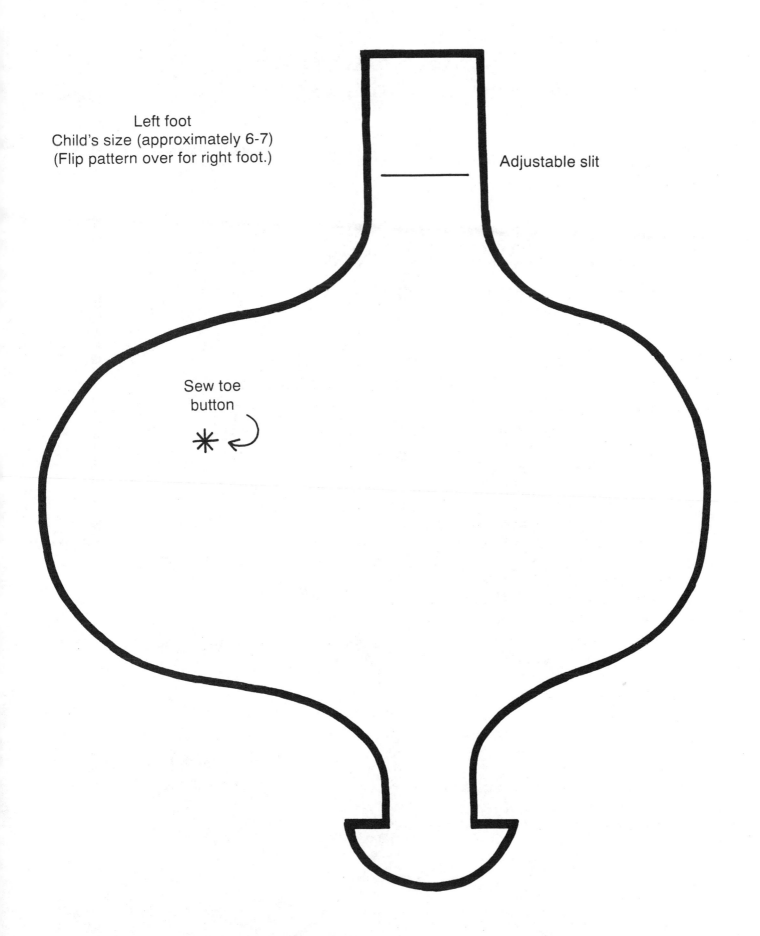

Left foot
Child's size (approximately 6-7)
(Flip pattern over for right foot.)

Adjustable slit

Sew toe
button

SS3823

Sweden

HEART BASKETS
Heart baskets for Christmas tree and treats

Christmas in Sweden is exciting. All the Swedish children make julgranskorgar (heart baskets) to be hung on the tree before the lights come on on Christmas Eve. These baskets are very easy to make!

MATERIALS:
Patterns (on this page)
Colored paper
Glue
Scissors
Pencil
Treats

Step 2

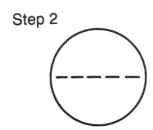

Step 3

INSTRUCTIONS:
1. Cut out pattern A. Trace one on two different colors of paper.
2. Cut out, then fold each circle in half.
3. Put the right piece inside the left one, folded sides out.
4. Glue between the overlapping edges.
5. Cut out pattern B. Trace it on a piece of paper, and cut out.
6. Glue to insides of basket to make a handle.
7. When the glue has dried, fill the basket with treats and hang it on your tree.

Step 5

Pattern B

VARIATION:
This design would be great for Valentine's Day or May Day.

BIBLICAL TEACHING:
Why not make some heart baskets and fill them with treats or gifts to give secretly to some people? Read Matthew 6:3-4.

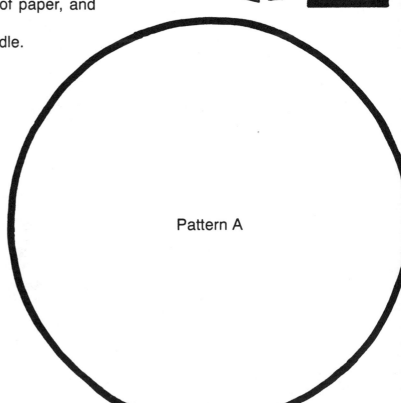

Pattern A

Switzerland

CANDLES
A candle that will give light but looks good enough to eat.

Switzerland is a country well-known for the beautiful Alps that cover 60 per cent of its land. It is also well-known for its yummy chocolate and holey cheese. With wax, ice cubes, and a few other things, you can make a candle that will remind you of delicious Swiss cheese.

MATERIALS:
16-ounce box of paraffin (found in supermarkets)
Old candle wicks or new wick string purchased at craft stores
Pencil
Half-pint milk carton
Orange or yellow crayons
Ice cubes

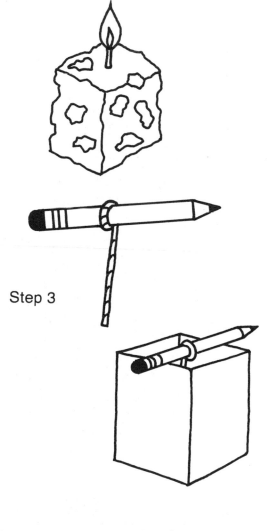

INSTRUCTIONS:
1. ADULT SUPERVISION NEEDED: Melt paraffin in a double boiler over medium heat.
2. Add one orange or yellow crayon to be melted in the paraffin. Stir well.
3. Tie wick around center of pencil. Hang wick in clean milk carton.
4. Fill carton with medium-sized ice cubes.
5. Pour wax into milk carton.
6. Let wax set completely. Pour off water; then tear away carton.
7. Untie pencil and trim wick to about 1".
Note: This recipe will make more than one candle.

Step 3

VARIATION:
Use a half-gallon milk carton instead.

BIBLICAL TEACHING:
God's Word, the Bible, is like a light for us. Through His Word the Lord guides us and shows us what to do. Read Psalm 119:105.

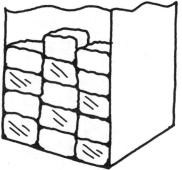

Step 4

Cutaway view

Syria

SAND POURING
Sand is grand!

Syria is a country on the eastern end of the Mediterranean Sea with fertile plains and mountains, but also large desert areas. With so much sand around, Syrians must have come up with many ways to use it creatively. Let's use a little creativity ourselves as we work with sand.

MATERIALS:
Sand
Paper cups
Water
Spoons
Food coloring or dry powdered fabric dye
Paper towels
Small glass jars with lids (such as baby food jars)
Paper clip

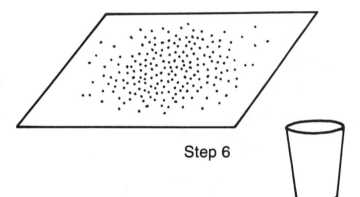

Step 6

INSTRUCTIONS:
1. Fill paper cups half full with sand.
2. Add water to cover sand in each cup.
3. Add drops of different colors of food coloring or powdered fabric dye to each cup.
4. Stir with a spoon.
5. Let the sand sit for fifteen minutes.
6. Pour out water. Spoon each cup of sand onto a separate paper towel to dry. Spread out.
7. After sand is dry, use spoons to fill jars layering different colors of sand. Last layer should come barely to neck of jar.
8. Open a paper clip to form a straight wire.
9. Experiment with shapes by poking clip in sand near sides of jar.
10. Replace lid after filling jar to top with extra sand.

Step 7

Step 8

Step 9

SAND PAINTING

MATERIALS:
Colored sand (Follow steps 1-6 of Sand Pouring project on page 94.)
Pencil
Margarine tub
Glue
Cotton swab or small paintbrush
Tagboard, cereal box cardboard, or heavy cardboard
White paper
Scissors

INSTRUCTIONS:
1. Cut cardboard to fit paper.
2. Glue paper to cardboard.
3. Draw picture.
4. Pour glue into tub.
5. Dip cotton swab or brush into glue and spread over an area in picture.
6. Sprinkle colored sand over glue.
7. Let dry; then tip paper to remove excess sand.

BIBLICAL TEACHING:
Look at some sand. This finely ground material was once rocks and shells. Over a long period of time, water wore them down into smooth, soft sand. When God created this world, He planned laws of nature that make everything work together, even to the finest details, like grains of sand. Read Colossians 1:16-17.

United States

LANTERNS
You are rich enough to work with poor man's silver.

Man has been working with tin since 3000 B.C. It has been combined with other metals since then. Pewter, a tin-lead alloy, was developed in the Middle Ages. In the American colonies, tin-plated iron was used as a less expensive material for craft work. It was called poor man's silver. Tin cans can easily be made into lanterns and candle holders much like those in the American colonies of the 1700s.

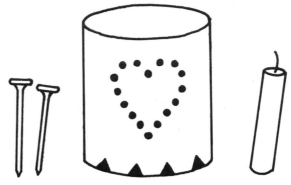

MATERIALS:
Tin cans of all sizes
Water
Nails
Hammer
Candle

INSTRUCTIONS:
1. Remove labels from cans by soaking them in warm water.
2. Fill can with water. Allow water to freeze completely overnight in your freezer.
3. Plan design you would like to make on the sides of tin can.
4. ADULT SUPERVISION NEEDED: When water is frozen, use nail and hammer to poke holes in special designs on can.
5. Allow ice to melt when you are finished.
6. Optional: Make holes with can opener on bottom of can for better air flow.
7. Secure candle at bottom of tin can.

BIBLICAL TEACHING:
A tin can isn't very attractive, even when you punch a design into it. But when you put a candle inside, the beauty of the light shines through and makes the can look beautiful. God wants to shine through our lives, making us beautiful because He is beautiful. Read Philippians 2:14-15.

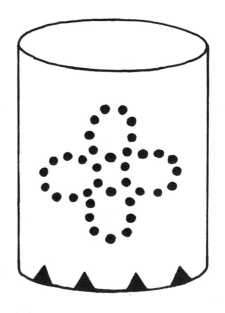